$5 ⁰⁰

CRIME

KIDNAPPED!

KIDNAPPED!
17 Days of Terror
by Curtis Bill Pepper

H

Harmony Books/New York

Harmony Books, a division of Crown Publishers, Inc.
One Park Avenue, New York, New York 10016

Published simultaneously in Canada by General Publishing
Co., Ltd. Printed in the United States of America.

Designed by Ken Sansone

Library of Congress Cataloging in Publication Data

Pepper, Curtis Bill.
    Kidnapped!

    1. Lazzaroni, Paolo. 2. Kidnapping—Italy—Case studies.
3. Italy—Social conditions. 4. Italy—Politics and government—1945-   I. Title.
HV6604.I82L396   1978   364.1'54'0926   78-14803
ISBN 0-517-53438-X

FOR: Paolo and Anna Lazzaroni, and many thousands like them, who live with the terror of kidnapping yet refuse to abandon their country in its hour of need, and...

FOR: Major Francesco Delfino and all carabinieri in the battle against organized crime —and finally for women of courage like Carla who bear witness to the heroic resolve of their men.

KIDNAPPED!

MONDAY
The 1st Day

IT HAPPENED when he least expected it, and it took only a few minutes.

He had driven his blue Alfetta 1800 out of the factory gate and onto a ramp curving into the Como-Milan highway—it was raining and cold, and he was off to Milan, a gym workout and home—when he noticed a car slow down in front of him. Then the car stopped, as though suddenly aware it had taken the wrong turn. Paolo Lazzaroni stopped behind it.

It was 6:58 P.M., Monday, March 21, 1977.

Paolo—a handsome man of forty, with a trim brown beard, hazel eyes and the light complexion of a Lombard—saw three men leap from the car. They wore dark hoods and carried machine guns. As they came toward him, he realized there was nothing he could do.

One of them opened the door and another yanked him out, yelling, "Get out! Out!" The third one opened the rear door of their car, and together they shoved him in, face down on the seat.

Then they were off. One of the men sat on his legs and poked a gun in his ribs. A second one crouched on the floor and began to put gauze over his eyes. Then he saw an injection needle, and panicked.

"Please," he begged them. "Don't give me drugs. I'm allergic. It will cause a violent reaction."

The gauze was fixed in place by a tape wound around his head. Blinded, he expected to feel the needle plunge into his body.

Then he heard a voice: "Okay, hold it for now."

Someone slipped a hood over his head, pulled his arms behind his back, and slapped on handcuffs.

"Listen, Lazzaroni, you do what we tell you and nothing will happen. But if you get smart, you'll get a bullet instead of a needle—got it?"

"Yes ... I got it."

Paolo Lazzaroni realized it would be two hours, at least, before anyone discovered he was missing. His wife, Anna, was with their children at a ski school in the mountains, where he had spent the weekend, returning to the factory only that morning. The maid at their home in Milan didn't expect him for dinner until 9 P.M. With the rain, his friends at the gym would think he'd gone elsewhere.

He could see the morning papers: "KIDNAP INC. GRABS SON OF BISCUIT KING." There would doubtless be a story on the family. For four generations, the Lazzaronis had made Italy's most prestigious cookies. Their amaretti were prized by the Queen of England, Japanese tea connoisseurs, French gourmets, New York's smartest caterers. Maybe there'd be a picture of their little steamship, *Esportazione,* now their trademark. There would certainly be the same list that appeared after every kidnapping—those who had been returned, and those who hadn't been.

There were all kinds of ways it could go badly. If you saw their faces. If the police bungled it. If your family failed to pay, or to play by the rules. You could end up like Cristina Mazzotti, lovely girl of eighteen, found buried under a garbage dump. They could also find you dead in a freshly dug grave under a fake tombstone. Or upright in the cement pylon of a luxury apartment building. Where was his own neighbor, Di Capua, seized in front of his home? His family had paid a huge ransom; yet he was believed to be dead.

It was incredible. Here they were in Lombardy, the richest region of the industrial north, with 18,000 corporations, a fifth of the number for all of Italy, producing 40 percent of the country's

GNP. They fancied themselves the smartest men in Italy. Yet a few dozen criminals were picking them off like fleas.

Look at the rest of Italy, for that matter. The biggest industries, like Montedison, going broke. Italians fleeing the country, taking $50 billion in lire with them. Ten million non-Marxists voting for the Communist party. One million unemployed university graduates filling the piazzas, some with painted faces, others with pistols and hand grenades. (Another way of masking their demand to be loved, to belong, to serve some cause that would give them an identity?) Why couldn't a civil service of 2 million employees deliver a letter on time or bury the dead before they piled up in stinking morgues in every corner of the country? The streets didn't belong to the people anymore. You couldn't walk them as you used to in Italy, as though they were outdoor living rooms—not without fear of mugging or rape or kidnapping. The whole society was unraveling. Why was Italy in this terrible mess—floundering as he was now in the rear seat of his own car, handcuffed and bound to darkness on a journey to the end of an unknown night?

The car turned off the highway into slower traffic. After many more turns, it stopped. "Quiet now," one of the men said, "or we'll kill you."

They pulled him out and carried him up two flights of stairs. They sat him down—on the edge of a bed, apparently—and searched him, taking away his driver's license, wallet, and address book. There was a sound of others entering the room.

"Lazzaroni, it's very simple. Do as we say, and you'll be all right. But if you don't, or if your family plays dirty, you'll never see them again." It was a new voice, hard, with a finality to it, like a northern Italian playing Humphrey Bogart playing a gangster. The other voices had been softer, with a Calabrian accent.

Paolo said he understood.

"Give us someone's name," Bogey said. "So we can tell him we've got you."

Paolo gave the names of his brother, Luigi; his father-in-law, the lawyer Aurelio Manzoni; and, if neither answered the phone, his sister, Pia. "My brother might have left the office. What time is it?"

"Eight-ten."

"Try him at home, too."

Eight-ten. Allowing fifteen to twenty minutes for the kidnapping, the stair-climbing and the delay in the room, he was forty to forty-five minutes' drive from the highway ramp behind his factory. They had to be somewhere in the outskirts of Milan.

There was the sound of men leaving. The handcuffs were painfully tight. He said, "Is there anyone here?"

"Yes. Me." The voice was a high-pitched falsetto, obviously disguised.

"My arms are swelling. Couldn't you loosen the handcuffs a bit?"

"I'm sorry, I don't have the key, and I must tell you it'll be two or three hours before they get rid of your car and make the calls."

The pain was getting worse. Something had to be done.

"If you get some cold water and rags, maybe it'll keep the swelling down."

This was done, and the constricted falsetto asked if he felt better.

"A little bit. If I need you, what's your name?"

"You can say Pippo and I'll know it's me."

"I appreciate your help, Pippo."

"It's nothing. I have to feed you, too. What do you eat?"

Paolo told him coffee with milk in the morning, maybe some veal and salad at midday, and cheese and fruit at night—a light diet to conform to his confinement.

"How do you cook veal?" Pippo asked.

"You put it in a pan, with butter. After a while, you turn it over."

"Okay, I got it. You know," Pippo added, almost plaintively. "I'm not a cook."

The pain was bad now. His hands and arms throbbed as though about to burst. He tried to think of something else, and his thoughts returned to Anna and the children in the mountains. He had promised to call tonight. She would be waiting for it. When it didn't come, she would call their home. Or else she would hear it on the radio in the morning—hopefully when the children were already out on the ski slopes. They had to be protected from this. They were too young for it.

OUTSIDE: By now, the family was alarmed. When Paolo failed to show for dinner, the maid called his mother, Augusta. She called Paolo's brother-in-law, Marco, who had come with him that morning from the mountains. Marco recalled Paolo saying he wanted to see a special film. So he ran off to the movie house to determine if he was there.

After abandoning Paolo's car on the Milan outskirts, the kidnappers began to make their calls.

First they tried Paolo's brother, Luigi—or Gigi, as he is called— but he was not at his office or at home. Then they tried the father-in-law, Avvocato Manzoni, only to find the phone was constantly busy with Manzoni's two sons, Marco and Luca, talking to their girl friends.

So they called Paolo's sister, Pia, and got her daughter, Anna Paola, age thirteen. Anna Paola has a mature voice and the kidnappers thought it was Pia.

"Listen, we have your young brother in our hands.... You're going to need three billion lire if you ever want to see him again."

Anna Paola, who has no young brother, was delighted with what she believed to be another of her school chum's jokes.

"Oh, you can keep him—he's not worth a hundred lire!" She laughed, and hung up.

The lawyer, Aurelio Manzoni, returned home shortly before midnight. His son Luca was waiting up for him and quickly told his father what had happened. Paolo was missing—he had not shown up for dinner. His maid called his mother. His mother didn't know where he was. They had asked the highway police to look for a wreck.

Just then the phone rang. Manzoni heard a smooth, Lombard voice.

"Are you Avvocato Manzoni, the father-in-law of Paolo?"
"Yes."
"Listen, we have Paolo with us. Don't worry, he's all right. But

if you want to see him again, get three billion lire ready. Three billion.... You understand?"

"Yes."

Three billion lire.... That was almost $3½ million.

"No tricks, Avvocato. No police. Talk to no one, or it'll go real bad for you and Paolo."

There was a ruffle on the phone. Manzoni remembers imagining a beard scraping across the receiver, as though the man speaking into it were sharing the instrument with someone.

"I'm your official caller," the man said. "Remember my voice. Don't talk to anybody else, unless they use the password."

"What is the password?"

"*'Rispondo, sono vivo.'*"

Manzoni shuddered at the words: "I reply, I am alive."

"Remember, Avvocato, if you work with the cops, Paolo will never come home. Also, we'll need another outside phone to call you without being bugged. We'll ask Paolo about that. Until tomorrow." He hung up.

The abrupt ending to their talk puzzled Manzoni until he later learned all calls had to be made in less than three minutes—minimal time needed for the police to locate the origin of the call.

An hour after the kidnapper's call, Manzoni received another call from the carabinieri, the national police. The caller identified himself as Major Francesco Delfino: he said he understood from the highway police that his son-in-law, Paolo Lazzaroni, was missing. He wanted the lawyer to come around to his office as soon as possible—and to bring with him Luigi (Gigi) Lazzaroni, Paolo's brother and general director of the family firm.

En route to the carabinieri headquarters on Via Moscova, Manzoni talked with Gigi about what they could say and do. The bandits had warned them not to go to the police, especially not to tell them anything. Yet how could he, a lawyer, not respect the forces of the law? This was not going to be pleasant—or easy.

The two men entered the main gate of the carabinieri command at 1:15 A.M. Aurelio Manzoni, sixty, short and stocky in a plain dark suit, walked with the sober air of a dedicated investment lawyer. Gigi Lazzaroni, forty-six, tall and fashionably tailored, moved with the grace and assurance of an upper-class Lombard—his features handsome, with prematurely white hair, the aquiline nose of his father, and hazel eyes which seemed to reflect a long-buried sadness.

They found Major Delfino seated behind his desk—a thickset man in a light blue suit, with a checkered tie, a Groucho Marx mustache, soft brown eyes, and a sad smile. A typical Calabrian, Manzoni decided. He'd bet those eyes could go suddenly cold. On the wall behind him was a large map of Milan, divided into quadrants, with various pins and lights.

"Well," he said, "so your Paolo is missing. What else do you know?"

Manzoni recalled the kidnappers' warning to say nothing. Yet now, having been called in.... He told the major about the call—and the kidnappers' threats.

Delfino smiled to show his sympathy. "Bravo, Avvocato. You understand it perfectly. I don't have to tell you anything. Just keep answering your phone, and we'll tell you what to do."

Manzoni knew that meant his phone would be tapped. In fact, every family phone would be bugged. He thought hard: The bandits needed a secret unbugged phone to work out the ransom. Somehow, they'd have to establish one, without Delfino knowing about it.

"I don't have to tell you, Avvocato, that private dealing with criminals is against the law." Again that sad smile. As though he knew what the lawyer was thinking.

Was it a warning? Or fraternal advice? Do whatever is necessary, but don't tell me?

As they left, there was one more word of caution—or was it another piece of advice?

"You realize, of course, that the attorney general's office will proceed to block all your assets to prevent you from paying a ransom."

Gigi Lazzaroni turned angrily upon the officer.

"That's inhuman and stupid. What do you expect us to do? What are you achieving? You're only driving us to friends, to borrow from them—or from banks, at enormous interest. The police should stop this kind of thing before it happens!"

The major couldn't agree more. There had to be more preventive action. More cooperation among the various forces of order—carabinieri, questura, local police, internal revenue, all working on their own, and often in competition. They needed a mastermind computer with everything in it, including voiceprints. As for those blocked funds.... The major reeled off some statistics.

Eighty percent of all kidnappings were pulled off by Sicilian, Sardinian, and Calabrian gangs controlled by the Mafia, with contracts elsewhere in Europe and in the American Mafia. The ransom money was laundered by a handful of shady Italian and Swiss banks at a 40 percent discount, then used for purchasing drugs or arms, or for legitimate investment. Only 5 percent of the kidnappings were political—the ransom money used to finance ultraleftist terror gangs like the Red Brigades. The remaining 15 percent was the work of young criminals; they'd settle for as little as 150 million lire in ransom, not much more than $170,000, a sum most any middle-class Milanese could raise under duress. The blocking of funds, Delfino explained, was mainly meant to make it difficult for the lower-class punks—hit the kidnapping industry at its weakest spot.

"What about the high-class ones?" asked Gigi. "How do we get money for them?"

"When that becomes urgent," said Major Delfino, cryptically, "there's generally an answer for it."

So there was a way to handle it, even though it meant the magistrate would have to look the other way—*alla Italiana.*

Despite this, Gigi became increasingly concerned in the car driving home.

"We have to learn more about this, how to go about it, how to handle these men. The major told us nothing.... What do you think of him?"

"Delfino? Very smart," replied Manzoni. "He's got the instinct of a jungle cat. Great cops and criminals all have it."

"We can't let him know what we're doing. We have to do this alone."

Manzoni agreed.

"Absolutely. In something like this, you trust no one outside your own family. We have to find a way to deal directly with these bandits and create a balance of belief or trust that will give us an operating basis."

"How can we ever trust them?"

"We can't, of course. Not all the way. But they have to feel they can trust us—that we'll keep our word. No frills, no tricks. Some hostages never come back, or their return is delayed for months, because the bandits thought they were being tricked and it was too risky to telephone. See what I mean? If they think we're working with Delfino, we can lose Paolo. For them a bullet in his head is nothing, compared to going to prison."

"So what'll we do?" asked Gigi.

"Prisco," replied Manzoni.

Avvocato Giuseppe Prisco, a close friend and president of the Milan Association of Lawyers, had agreed to help any Lazzaroni if kidnapped.

"Yes, Prisco," agreed Gigi. "Paolo will surely have them call him. He's already in contact with Di Capua's kidnappers and he knows how to handle these people. Yes ... if anybody can outsmart Delfino, it's Prisco."

"Maybe," replied Manzoni. "But I wouldn't be too sure. Did you read about him in today's papers? Very impressive. He's no ordinary cop."

WATCHING THE TWO MEN leave, Major Delfino felt a pang of sorrow for them. And, for some reason, for himself. It really had to do with something else. Italy, perhaps. Everybody in the whole damn world, except maybe some Eskimos and cannibals, had dunked Lazzaroni amaretti in their tea cups. Now this *rapimento* was going to be plastered all over the papers, from New York to Tokyo. More magazine covers with spaghetti and a *pistola*. Those Italians again. Never could govern themselves.

Ecco, la bella Italia! Sure, but it wasn't that much better anywhere else these days. Try and walk around New York at night. Hell, you could get yourself gunned down in Bonn in broad daylight. Or kidnapped anywhere in France or Switzerland.

Yet Italy had always been first in most everything. Maybe it was the sun, the sea, or the ancient land—whatever caused it, Italians seemed destined to be a social laboratory for the rest of Europe. It wasn't only being first with the Roman Empire. Italians were also first to eat with knives and forks, before the French copied them. They were first with codified modern law. First with National Socialism—which was copied by Germany. First to recover from that political disaster with the "Italian miracle" of the 50s. First with the economic sag of the 60s. Now first with this civic terror of the 70s.

In Lombardy, especially, kidnapping had become a major industry, averaging 1 million dollars for one kidnap each month—double the sum paid in all the rest of Italy. No wonder. All those Mafia big shots in the south, exiled by the courts to northern Italy—it was like sending mice from the kitchen to the cheese pantry. Lombardy was a paradise for them. They all worked together—Sicilian Mafia, Calabrian *'ndrangheta,* some Sardinians as well. The men who grabbed Lazzaroni were probably already back in Calabria, sitting in a piazza, sipping white wine. Those who did the actual kidnappings left the guard duty and the negotiating to others.

He looked at his watch: 1:40 A.M. Time to close shop and go home. It'd been some day—his first as new commander of Milan's Nucleo Investigativo, the anticrime squad. Clearing his desk, he found some unread news clippings reporting his arrival as part of the city's stepped-up drive against growing crime.

The stories indicated Major Delfino was no ordinary cop. One paper called him an "Italian Kojak"—from the popular American TV show, currently running in Italy. The bare facts revealed an extraordinary career. Born at Plati, heartland of the Calabrian Mafia, or *'ndrangheta* ... son of a famous carabiniere bandit hunter ... he rose quickly in rank to graduate from the Accademia Militare at Modena, whose discipline and training rivals Saint Cyr or West Point ... out of ninety-five applicants for twenty-five posts, only sixteen managed to finish.... Studied nights to obtain a doctorate in political science from the University of Cagliari with a thesis on kidnapping ... a second doctorate in judicial law, University of Parma, with a thesis on international drug traffic ...

for courage and bravery in capturing bandits and terrorists, three silver-star decorations for valor. No carabiniere in history had received such honors nor been so promoted in peacetime, passing over 180 other captains to become major.

It was all there—only it wasn't. Not the reality of it, not how it had been, nor how it was even now. The long years, like a worn trail over the rocky mountains of Calabria, the face and hands of his father in the coffin, the grave with the bowed heads of the men he had hunted. Then, later, the endless army barracks of men lost in time, the dark landscape of violence and death, secret encounters in mountain caves, in cruising cars and dark alleys—the lies, betrayals, sudden gunfire, the haunted eyes of both his men and the others, the fear and then from nowhere the sudden courage.... And all of it with Carla always there, waiting for him, holding their children, asking him, "Did I cry again in my sleep?" while he lied, as he always did in this, "No, you were quiet, like a sleeping princess." Who could understand it? How could anyone know how it really was? That night in Sardinia, returning from a raid, his arm bleeding from a wound, finding Carla about to give birth to Andrea: "You're wounded, Franco." "No, it's nothing." And she: "Let me help you ..." but then she couldn't because the baby began to come. As they took her away, she cried out to him: "Why? Why does it have to be this way, Franco? Why can't we live like other people? Why?...WHY?"

The phone rang on the private line. He picked it up, knowing that at this hour it had to be Carla, sleepily calling from their bed to make sure he was all right.

"Maggiore Delfino?"

"Speaking."

Quickly, he punched the recording button.

"I'm Antonio."

"Yes, I know."

"I must see you. Urgent."

"Okay, noon tomorrow. The usual place."

"No, not there. I don't trust it anymore."

"Where then? Tell me."

"I don't know. I'll call you when I get to town."

"You got some new ones?"

"New ones and something else. The connection."

"The big one?"

"*Si,* Signore."

"Does it go up toward the top?"

"Right up—to the big ones we've been looking for...."

There was a pause. When Antonio spoke again, it sounded like he was behind a counter in a store.

"So how many forms you want? You have to tell me. I can't haul around a lot of cheese forms for nothing."

Porco cane. Someone must have come near the phone. So now Antonio was talking about his damn cheeses. It was probably his wife, who didn't know he was an informer.

"How much you want? The same number? Okay. Tomorrow about noon."

"I got you," replied Delfino. "Until tomorrow noon."

Madonna, was it possible? Antonio sounded like he had found the link to the whole network—right up to Mr. Goldfinger of the new Mafia, sitting in a luxurious villa amidst many other villas where his victims lived, unaware that the source of the primal evil lived in their midst, was a member of their clubs, and occasionally sat at their dinner tables...

The phone rang again. This time it was a reporter from *Corriere della Sera,* speaking above the din of teleprinters and typewriters. What could the major tell them about Paolo Lazzaroni? Delfino explained there was nothing concrete, other than a phone call from the bandits confirming they had Paolo in custody.

"We understand that call was made to Avvocato Manzoni and they asked for three billion lire."

"Who told you that?"

There was a pause which irritated Delfino.

"Listen, if you want straight talk, why don't you try it yourself?"

"It was the brother, Luigi, who spoke to one of our editors just now. He asked us not to reveal it."

"So why bother me?"

"We've been trying to figure this out. In the last three days, between Rome and Milan, there've been three major kidnappings, plus the return of two hostages from earlier ones. Does this indicate that Lazzaroni has a two out of three chance to come home alive?"

"It depends on who grabbed him."

"The last two hostages apparently paid over two billion lire in ransom. Isn't that some kind of record?"

"I don't know," replied Delfino, again irritated. "But it can't last. Sooner or later, we'll get the whole damn lot of them."

"If they don't get you first—right?"

"What do you mean?"

The reporter explained that Fernando Pomarici—an assistant attorney general who specialized in kidnapping—had received anonymous threats against himself and his family.

"So we assume they've also threatened you, Signor Maggiore."

"I don't know what you mean."

He didn't want to talk about it. Every cop or judge or lawyer received threats. Even journalists received them. If you fought criminals, you received them. It was part of the business. But you didn't talk about it, and he doubted that Pomarici had talked.

"Why are you asking me this?"

"It seems to be important in this kidnap boom. Scare hell out of the judges and the police. Back it up by killing them every so often, especially the ones who get too close...."

"I never think about it.... Goodnight," replied Delfino, hanging up.

He opened the top drawer of his desk, took out a Colt .38 pistol, jammed it into a belt holster, and left his office.

In the courtyard of the *caserma,* he got behind the wheel of his Alfa-Romeo 1800 and drove out past the guarded gate, alone through dark streets toward his apartment in a large palazzo in Via Marcora which also contained the command center of the 1st Carabiniere Division for North Italy.

Twice, as he halted for a stoplight, another car pulled up close to his. Out of habit, his hand moved toward his Colt .38 while glancing at the driver. If he continued to penetrate the Mafia— especially now with Antonio uncovering links inside Kidnap Inc.—

it could happen this way at a stoplight, any hour of the night. Or even during the day. You had to learn to live with it. His father had done it and he had become a legend. And now he was going to do it as his father had done it—going to the end, whatever that would be.

Still, that reporter had been right. It was a new ball game now. In his father's time, no one would have considered killing a carabiniere. His father had hunted bandits, but they had never hunted him. Now it was different. The days of his father were finished. With the new Mafia, no public office or life was sacred.

Increasing numbers of carabinieri and other agents were being murdered—or crippled for life. Last week in Rome, Public Security agent Cesare Onofri had been shot in the spine, leaving his legs paralyzed for life. Another agent, Domenico Arboretti hit in the brain, was left semiparalyzed without the power of speech—instant old age in a young man's body. Nobody was safe from it—not even a colonel in the carabinieri. Giuseppe Russo had been murdered while taking a stroll near Corleone, then left there—his head on the sidewalk, his body in the gutter, like a run-over dog. Violent death robbed you twice.

He parked his car before the large carabiniere building. At the entrance, he was saluted by a guard who gave him two messages. One was from Avvocato Giuseppe Prisco, asking the major to call him early in the morning. Was it about Paolo Lazzaroni? Perhaps. The lawyer was already serving as a liaison between three families with kidnap victims. One of them, Di Capua, was a neighbor of Paolo Lazzaroni.

Tomorrow he would request the phone taps on the Lazzaronis to include their close friends and whomever might be used as a phone contact with the kidnappers. Manzoni was too exposed for the job. The newspapers already knew too much about him. Most likely it would be Prisco.

The second message was from Antonio. It contained one word: *urgente,* and the hour of the call: 1:30 A.M. So he had called here first, before the office. Obviously, Antonio was on to something big—probably the biggest thing yet. Bigger than the capture of the Sicilian bandit, Roberto Campana. Bigger than the massacre of civilians at Piazza della Loggia. Bigger than the Brescia MAR Fascist roundup—or even the capture of the Red Brigades leader, Giorgio Semeria.

This led to the operational command of the kidnap industry in Lombardy—and from there to the heart of the Mafia in Italy. Somewhere, on some lower level, in some dark room, Paolo Lazzaroni lay waiting for release.

TUESDAY
The 2nd Day

HE AWOKE with a sense of being buried alive. There was a moment of panic—then he remembered. His arms and wrists still ached, but his hands were manacled in front of him.

The other men, returning after midnight, had relented. Even old Bogey had sounded less mean, though he warned Paolo that if he used his handcuffed hands to remove his eye tape they would kill him. There was also another man to stand guard with Pippo, who disguised his voice as a basso, similar to Bogey's.

Paolo had asked for the toilet and had been given a chamber pot. With his hands manacled and his eyes blinded, he had managed to squat onto it. That, too, would be part of his daily humiliation.

How long could he endure this darkness, this airlessness? Especially since he had always felt a compulsive need for fresh air? His panic returned—a sudden rush of fear, binding him within it and growing in intensity until he thought he could take no more. At that moment, it seemed to break apart and he was free.

The panic left him and he felt an immense calm. It was overwhelming, and he wondered where it had come from. He had read reports of people who died—ceased to live in medical terms—

and then came back to life. They all said that at the moment of dying there is an enormous serenity that cancels all panic and gives the individual the courage to resume life—or to release it—in the last moments left to him.

This was happening to him now. Yet he didn't see himself as dead or tortured or an object of violence. He had been seized by an impersonal force. Before him were certain alternatives. He could take whatever alternative seemed the most conducive to surviving, or at least to functioning in a tranquillity he had never imagined possible under such circumstances.

He realized he was witnessing the potential of the human mind to save itself. It lay deep within the brain, untouched and unknown until it was needed. Eventually it appeared and took control, as it was doing now, creating an insulating space between his body and the dangers before it—allowing him the time and the clarity to best decide on how to save himself.

With this calm, he began to plan his first day. Lying in the dark, he could order his hours and thoughts—and so be free. He could retrace his trips to Amazonia, to India, to Uganda ... and his honeymoon with Anna.

"You want some breakfast?"

It was Pippo, speaking with his squeezed-up voice. Paolo accepted the coffee with milk and a roll, then had another go on the chamber pot.

Later in the morning, Bogey returned. He said they needed another contact besides Manzoni. Paolo recalled Avvocato Prisco's offer to help them in event of kidnapping, and he gave Bogey the lawyer's name.

They left him then, and he began to do isometric exercises while trying to imagine what Prisco, Gigi, and Anna would be telling Bogey and his men.

OUTSIDE: Gigi had not slept all night. After leaving Major Delfino, he realized that Paolo's chances depended upon their being better informed and more organized. There was no time to rest. Minutes counted.

First, he called an editor of *Corriere della Sera,* who was a friend, and told him of the kidnapping, which had occurred after the paper's last edition. He asked a personal favor: "In tomorrow's paper, please don't headline Paolo as son of a biscuit king, or say we're millionaires, because other papers will copy you and the kidnappers will be less inclined to bargain with us. They're asking three billion lire and we can never meet it, unless we sell the company." The editor sleepily agreed to do what he could.

Next, Gigi awakened Alberto Alemagna, another pastry king, whose seven-year-old son, Daniele, had been kidnapped and released on payment of a billion lire. "Tell me, Alberto, what to do. How do we deal with these people?"

After listening to Alemagna, he called three others who had had relatives kidnapped and returned. Each one had a different story, but there were points in common: Make sure they actually have the hostage; don't use your own telephone; limit all calls to less than three minutes; read from a prepared text, so you don't slip in a wrong or angry word; seek to understand bandit psychology and to gain their confidence; be cautious with the press, the local police, and the carabinieri.

Gigi then awakened the Lazzaronis' administrator and told him to be sure to withdraw the family's entire liquid assets and place them in a safe-deposit vault.

At 6 A.M., he phoned Dottore Agostino Vanelli, seventy-four, family doctor for forty years, asking him to be present when he broke the news to his eighty-two-year-old father, Mario.

The doctor came with a heart stimulant. As they entered the living room, the old man was listening to the seven o'clock news. He looked up, his face working.

"Povera Italia, poveri noi," he said. "Poor Italy, poor us."

Mario Lazzaroni, who has white hair and the features of an aging eagle, was still active at the plant. His response to the kidnapping was to leave for work early, to take Paolo's place.

Gigi hurried on to tell his father's sister, Ernesta, but she already knew. He found her in the garden, seated in a chair, weeping without words. After that, he returned to his own home and found his ten-year-old son, Giulio, also in tears. He comforted his child, but the fright and sadness remained. A kidnapping was a double crime.

It was getting late: 8:10 A.M. He had to tell Manzoni what he had learned before the bandits called again. After that, he was due at the factory to call a meeting of their salesmen who had begun a slowdown strike for a greater percentage of sales.

The kidnappers' second call came at 9 A.M. Aurelio Manzoni was in court, but his son Marco had been primed by Gigi on what to say.

After hearing the password—*"Rispondo, sono vivo"*—he was asked if the Lazzaronis were getting the ransom ready? Yes, he replied, they were trying to raise it. And, as proof that Paolo was actually their prisoner, would they—the next time they called— please relay the names of Paolo and Anna's closest friends in America?

Thereafter, this became a ritual with each call. First the password, then a reply to a previous question (which only Paolo could answer), then a new question for the next call. After that, they would talk about the ransom.

This morning, however, there was nothing more. The Caller, as he named himself, seemed angry and hung up.

AT THE SKI SCHOOL in the Alps near Sestriere, Paolo's wife, Anna, had been worried since the previous evening. Paolo had not called her from Milan, as promised. Shortly before breakfast, she finally heard about it. The children's ski teacher came running into the chalet, her face dark and sad.

"Oh, Anna! They've got Paolo! They kidnapped him."

She left the children—Luca, five, and Marco, three—with her friends at the chalet, to continue their ski training and to isolate them from whatever terrors lay ahead.

In the car, driving to Milan, she tried to think of what to do. But she could think of nothing except Paolo and how much she loved him.

She recalled one day, during their honeymoon in Uganda, when their car was stuck in the sand and she had been trying to help dig it out. Bending over, she felt dizzy and suddenly realized, in the middle of Africa, that she was pregnant. She had said nothing, waiting until they had reached camp and their Ugandan guide, Justice—renamed by baptizing Christian missionaries—had served them drinks. She had told him then. When she saw his happiness, she had cried with joy, and there were tears in his eyes, too, as he took her in his arms....

What, she wondered, did that memory mean? That she was going to have to dig Paolo out, without fainting? Get better control of herself? Maybe it was that, because he was going to need her more than anybody else. Wherever he was, he was counting on her to get him out. Where would it be? In a cellar somewhere? Chained to a bed like a dog? No, *Signore mio,* help me not to think that way.

She saw him then, as he had been when they first met in his mother's garden, that summer afternoon, under the old cloister columns. She wore a turquoise dress, her blond hair pulled back in a chignon, while he stood before her, smiling and saying, "I never expected you to look like this."

In that instant, looking into his eyes and hearing his voice, she was overwhelmed with feelings she had never had before. They had just met, yet she instinctively knew what he was like, just as he knew who she was. Without being aware of it, she had been searching for another part of herself, a missing part, and finally she had found it in him.

They were alike in many ways, yet different in ways that gave them strength and brought them happiness. She, for example, tended at times to be depressed and pessimistic. Paolo was optimistic when she was not, which helped her. Also, he was a *bel romantico.* He remembered special dates and emotional moments that can mean so much to a woman. He also had a way of touching her or looking at her across a dinner table with a little smile that said, simply, "Hello, love."

She was more realistic. She had a faster mind. She could see one, two, three things at a time. Perhaps this was also a defect of some women: to get lost in details and miss the long view. Paolo had that. Yet now he was counting on her to have the vision to find him and to bring him home. That's what he expected and nothing would stop her, nothing....

THE MANZONI PHONE rang again that evening, shortly after 10 P.M. Once more, Marco answered. The Caller gave the password, then the correct reply to the morning's question: "The American friends are called Matt and Ellen."

Marco asked a question for the next call: The name of a former nanny for their children.

"Okay. Now, whom do we talk to about the money?"

Marco said he thought it was Avvocato Prisco. The Caller said they'd tried to reach the *avvocato* but weren't doing very well. Marco said he'd try to find out why.

"Listen, smart boy, is this phone bugged?"

Marco said he didn't think so. The man hung up.

THE PLAYBACK ENDED and Major Delfino snapped off his phone link with the telephone recording center.

Very interesting. A short conversation, but right to the point. The bandits wanted to prove that Paolo was alive. They wanted to start talking about ransom payment. And they wanted a secret phone. They knew Manzoni's phone was tapped. The question was actually a way of telling Manzoni that they knew it—and to get moving.

Until they located a phone which they believed was untapped by the police, the calls from the gang would be like that one—tough, nervous, and meant to frighten. After they found it, the kidnappers would continue to make calls on the same tapped lines, but it would be playacting for the cops' benefit, and you'd know it immediately.

The Caller had a Milanese accent, but it was once more the same sort: A second-generation Calabrian or Sicilian. And very savvy. Paolo Lazzaroni was lucky. This was a professional gang, not some street punks trying to break into the big time. You had a better chance with the pros.

Christ, he'd heard so many of these phone calls, he could write the script. First, the family is told to get the money and not talk to the cops. If they needed prodding, they'd get a fingertip by parcel post. If that wasn't enough, they'd get a whole finger or an ear. When there was a postal strike or a mix-up in the mail, these bits of human bodies often arrived two weeks or a month later—dried up, the flesh yellow, the blood dark brown.

The family now had to find a secret phone contact. Prisco was out of it. Somehow, the morning papers had named him as an intermediary for the Lazzaronis. That blew it. No kidnapper would ever call Prisco now, except for show.

Despite this, the lawyer was a family friend—and worried. When Delfino had returned his call that morning, Prisco noted that the family of Vittorio Di Capua, another kidnap victim, had paid the agreed ransom—close to $1.5 million in lire—only to be asked for another million.

That was a bad sign. It meant Di Capua was probably dead. Did Delfino think the same gang had Paolo Lazzaroni? Delfino had replied he didn't know, but thought not. Merely a hunch, he had told the lawyer. Nothing more.

Yet he had expected something much more important—without luck. Antonio had not phoned. That was very bad. When a top informant failed to show, you could count on trouble. And with this one, it could mean serious trouble—for all of them.

Gianfranco Gorgoni

bove: Paolo Lazzaroni and his wife, Anna.
elow: Paolo (left), his father, and his brother, Luigi (right), at the Lazzaroni factory.

Gianfranco Gorgoni

Gianfranco Gorg

Above: The Lazzaroni factory.

Right: Lazzaroni Amaretti biscuits with their trademark, the little steamship *Esportazione*.

aolo's car abandoned by the kidnappers. **Above:** Note empty spool for tape used to bind
im in blindness for 17 days.

Giancarlo De Be[

Above: Major Francesco Delfino of the Italian national police with plainclothesmen.
Below: Delfino, (right), called the "Italian Kojak," conferring with his assistants.

Giancarlo De B[

ni è nelle mani dei bandit
to un riscatto di 5 miliard

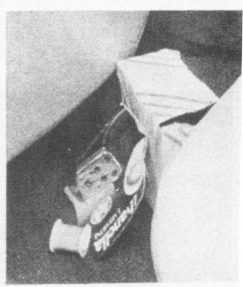

ewspaper headlines all over Italy announced the kidnapping of Paolo Lazzaroni.

Right: This picture was taken by the men who kidnapped Paolo Lazzaroni. It was sent by secret means to Anna to prove that her husband was still alive. The dark glasses were placed over Paolo's eyes to conceal the tape that sealed them shut. The Milan newspaper proves the date; the word "Justus" was the kidnappers' password.

Below: On the back of this Polaroid photo, taken by the kidnappers to prove that he was still alive, Paolo Lazzaroni wrote the name of the honeymoon isle, Nossi-be, where he and Anna spent many happy days.

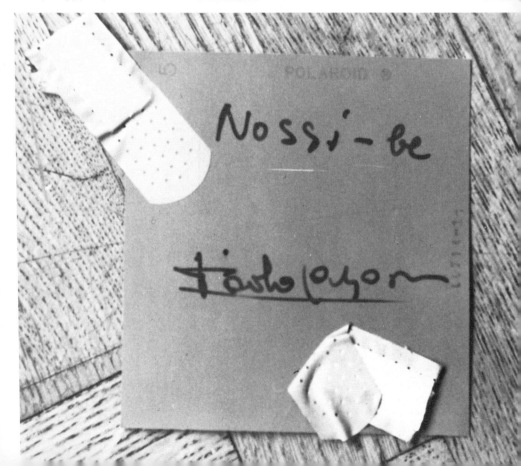

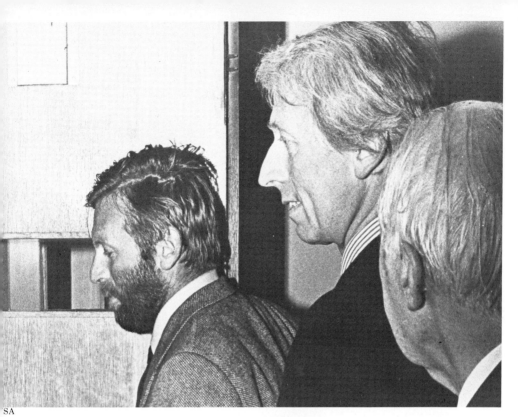

SA

Above: Paolo Lazzaroni (left) with his brother, Luigi, after his 17-day ordeal had ended. He was released when his family paid almost $1 million in ransom.

Left: Paolo Lazzaroni shown here smiling happily a few days after his release from the kidnappers.

ANSA

The Lazzaroni family reunited.

WEDNESDAY
The 3rd Day

PAOLO WOKE UP early and for a while lay in bed with his eyes closed, trying to listen for voices in the other room—voices without fake falsettos or bassos. He heard some movement and the morning news on the radio—too faint to make it out. His arms ached less, but he was beginning to smell—no bath and that stinking chamber pot.

Pippo brought breakfast and after that Paolo began his daily ritual. First, the isometric exercises—the legs, the abdomen, the arms. The handcuffs weren't bad for that. You could pull against them until the muscles ached, then up and down ... feeling the blood flowing.

After that, he was allowed to get up and sit in a wooden chair. He tried to imagine what Anna, Gigi, and Aurelio might be saying to these men. He had to be careful not to contradict them. They had never told him how much they were asking, or how the talks were going. It was important to convince them of the truth—that the Lazzaroni family consistently turned its earnings back into the factory. The rising cost of labor required continual replacement of newer and faster machines. Also, stocks had piled up, which was a form of capital drawing no interest.

Other industrialists had paid ransoms of more than a billion lire. Gianni Bulgari, they said, paid 10 billion—more than 11 million dollars. Where would the Lazzaronis get that kind of money? If they sold the firm, it would kill his father. It would be the end of a century of great enterprise. No ... never that. Someone had to convince them there wasn't that much money, certainly not as much as they were probably asking.

Somehow, he had to win their confidence, figure out what Gigi and Anna would offer, and suggest that sum to them as the limit of the possible.

Bogey came into the room with his false growl.

"Listen, your Avvocato Prisco is in the papers as your contact. So he's burnt out. Also Manzoni, but we'll use him anyway, to keep the cops scribbling happily. Now we need another name, someone you can trust, and we can trust, too. This is your neck, Mister. We're not playing games. Who you got?"

"Let me think."

He couldn't ask friends with children, or those with well-known names, to get mixed up with criminals. It was against the law—and risky, if they were rich. Also, it had to be someone who could go to his home and see Anna without arousing suspicion. Most likely his phone was tapped and policemen were in front of the house.

A priest. A priest would be ideal. There were two chaplains he had known when he was a radar specialist in the air corps, but they were not in Milan. Then there was Don Salvatore, his confidant at Collegio San Carlo. That was the man. During the war, Padre Salvatore had helped many Italians escape to Switzerland. He had courage. He was a little old now, maybe seventy, but he would do it.

Bogey liked the suggestion. "Not bad."

"It's very good," said Pippo, anxious to please.

The second guard, who spoke in a contrived basso, didn't want any part of it.

"Priests bring bad luck."

"Touch your balls," replied Pippo. "If you can find them."

"Don't get smart," said Basso, offended. "You can touch them all day long, but it won't help against priests."

"Shut up," growled Bogey. "You're talking like two women."

OUTSIDE: The day began with a shock for Anna. Marco Manzoni had a friend whose uncle had been kidnapped by mistake. The bandits thought he was a steel king when actually he was only a pig-iron merchant. No matter: They wanted money or else they'd start sending him back in installments. Finally they were paid and the uncle was set free.

The nephew came to Anna's in the morning and played the tapes of phone talks with the kidnappers. Anna was shocked at what she heard. It was so cold-blooded—as if they were arguing about the price of scrap iron, rather than a human life: "Look, *amico*, we can't afford it. We'll go broke. Come on, be a friend, try and understand." *Amico?* Friend? With those people? *Dio*, how awful! Yet how else were you going to do it?

Afterward, the nephew, a very competent young man, gave her the basic rules: Start your bids low; keep your word; build up confidence; don't get excited; write out your messages in advance; no family members as phone contacts (they get too excited); and as few people as possible making decisions.

That evening, Anna summoned the entire family to the Manzoni home, where the nephew replayed the tapes. The lesson was clear to everyone. It was decided to form a triumvirate to handle all future dealings: Gigi, Anna, and Aurelio Manzoni. They would meet nightly in Aurelio's law office, take common council, and coordinate plans for the following day. Also, Aurelio would ask the newspapers to help them by publishing as little as possible about the case—hoping in this way to obtain some calm in which to easily bargain with the kidnappers.

The bugged Manzoni phone would continue to be used as a cover for the police. In its place, they had to find another one—a secret line, unknown to anyone.

IT WAS AFTER MIDNIGHT when Delfino got a report of the meeting, with names of everyone attending. He grinned. Here was a very sensible family. They were handling it like a major sales campaign for cookies. No wonder the Lazzaronis had the clout to sell biscuits to the British. Typical Lombards. No nonsense. Give them a problem and they'll go at it.

They were probably trying to figure out how to find a safe phone but couldn't think of one that wasn't, in all likelihood, already tapped. Very frustrating. When would they realize that Paolo would have to find it for them?

This was the second meeting of the day for the wife, Anna. She was in the middle of it now, and moving faster than any of the others....

He recalled Antonio? Had they caught him? Madonna, anything but that. A car wreck. In bed with pneumonia. Anything, except being caught. If there was no word by tomorrow, they'd have to begin a search.

THURSDAY
The 4th Day

AFTER FINISHING his exercises, Paolo sat in the wooden chair, feeling relaxed. Old Don Salvatore was a perfect solution. All would go well now.

With that decided, he began one of his various "escapes" from the dark prison of the room. This morning he was back at Caprera, at the sailing school. The harbor had a narrow opening and there was a high wind, making it difficult to go beyond the outer rocks. There were many maneuvers to make, using a small Vaurien. He was running with the wind toward the rocks and about to turn about....

"That priest was a disaster."

"What?"

It was Bogey, entering the room with someone else.

"I said your priest isn't worth a fig. He's an idiot."

"My old friend, Padre Salvatore?"

"He ain't no friend of yours," said Basso, the second guard.

Upon learning Paolo was being held for ransom, the priest had yelled at them: "You can't do that to him!" They had tried to calm him, but he had continued his tirade: "You can't do that to anybody!...Don't you people have any conscience?"

"So we told him," said Bogey, "if we had any conscience we

wouldn't be in this racket, and hung up. You'd better get somebody who makes more sense. And get him fast, if you want to go home alive."

Paolo thought about it, eliminating one friend after another. Finally it came down to one man—a friend of both his and Anna's.

Bogey was gone, and he called in Pippo, telling him to look up the phone number in his pocket address book. When Pippo found it, Paolo told him to tell Bogey this was their man: Renzo ———.

OUTSIDE: At home, Anna called the mountain chalet to talk to her children. Luca excitedly told her he had skied down the medium slope. Marco chimed in to say he had done it, too, but the last half was on the seat of his pants. Franca Devecchi, their instructress and a family friend, told Anna not to worry—all was well. The children would soon be champions in their class. Also, they were making new friends.

Anna asked to speak to them again to say goodnight. Luca, who was five, grabbed the phone first.

"Mommie? Next week I can go on the real big slope!"

"All right, if they let you. But I don't think you should take Marco there. Are you taking care of your little brother?"

"Yes, here he is."

There was no sound and Anna knew Marco, who was only three, was holding the phone while waiting for her voice.

"Hello, little love."

"Hello."

He sounded so small and lost. He missed her. She knew he was very lonely without her.

"Little love, I'll come and see you soon."

"All right."

"I miss you, Marcolino."

"Yes, Mommie."

"You miss me?"

"No ... I mean, yes."

"Here's a kiss goodnight."

She kissed the phone and heard kisses on the other end, then their happy shouts: "Goodnight, Mommie!"

She cried then, sitting on the edge of her bed—imagining her boys hugging the phone and kissing it as though it were their mother. The innocence of children was so precious, so over-whelming—and so vulnerable. What could she tell them if Paolo never came home? How could she ever bring herself to look into their eyes?

She took a long, hot bath—hoping it would make her drowsy. But once in bed, she was unable to sleep. There had been no calls all day. She lay in the dark, trying to imagine what else she could do. Maybe if she tried hard enough to keep her mind pried open, maybe she would receive a message from Paolo. She had read of such things....

Nothing came to her. Yet she felt herself being transformed. She was a normal woman, like a million others. But this was changing her. The tension, the terror, the fright had fused her into ... into something outside herself, or maybe inside herself, without need to eat or sleep as she went on and on.

She began to pray to God through the Madonna of Lourdes, to whom she felt especially close after accompanying many infirm pilgrims to the famous shrine.

"*Signore,* keep him well. *Signore,* give him the strength to survive. And give me the strength to go on."

And then, to her own surprise: "*Signore,* forgive them, for they know not what they do. Help them, too."

After that, she felt sleepy. As she was drifting off, she thought of a name. He was an important businessman, and both he and his wife were trusted friends. They lived alone, without children or relatives. He would make an ideal contact for the kidnappers. Tomorrow she would ask him: "Caro Renzo, will you help us to bring Paolo home?"

MAJOR DELFINO had dined at his favorite pizzeria with Carla and their two children—Stefania, thirteen, and Andrea, eleven. Returning home, he found there had been no calls, no messages from the recording center.

So the bandits hadn't phoned the Lazzaronis all day—at least not on any of the tapped lines. Maybe they were already haggling over ransom terms on an unknown phone. Good. The sooner they started the better. It wouldn't be hard to locate the phone. The wife was in the middle of everything. She would lead them to it.

But still no word about Antonio was bad news. Real bad. He'd left home two days ago—and disappeared. They had searched for him everywhere—hospitals, city morgue, the usual hangouts, and finally the cafe where they occasionally met. Not a trace anywhere.

Without doubt, the underworld had grabbed Antonio—one of his best sources. To fight crime, you needed informants, and he had built up his own network. It required a lot of work and much personal risk. Very often he had to go into isolated areas, without full protection, because the informer trusted no one else and set his own conditions for the meeting. It was part of the job, and when you got a good man you tried to keep him.

Antonio had had Mafia members on both sides of his family, other relatives in the *'ndrangheta*—and an undying hatred for what they'd done to his sister. Informers often came to you that way—out of revenge. Or from pride, or for money, or to get rid of an enemy. Once they started talking, you could keep them going if you gave them sufficient incentive and covered their identity. But someone had uncovered Antonio—poor guy.

And poor Lazzaroni. Antonio probably had known where he was being hidden—or would have found it out. He had already helped them to find two other kidnap hideouts. They had been able to give the password in Calabrian dialect—then walk in, arrest the guards, and free the hostage.

But more than Lazzaroni, Antonio apparently had discovered some important figures in a kidnap network they were beginning to identify. To date, they had twenty-nine names, with more to come. Until he had them, Delfino was withholding the arrests.

His father, Maresciallo Delfino, had made the greatest Mafia roundup in history—110 top leaders gathered in a meeting on the summit of Monte Alto in the Calabrian mountains. And now, this operation in Milan would do honor to his father. Maybe—who knew?—it would lead them to the boss of bosses in Kidnap Inc. Sooner or later, they would find him.

FRIDAY
The 5th Day

SAY, PAOLO."

"Yes, Pippo?"

After serving him breakfast, Pippo seemed to want to talk. He had called him Paolo for the first time.

"When I was looking for your friend's number ... "

"Yes?"

"I saw the word *drugs* written in many places."

"Yes."

"Are you onto the stuff?"

"No, I'm helping others get off it." He explained that the Rotary and Lions Clubs of Milan had a joint program to combat the use of drugs and to rehabilitate addicts.

"You can make a pile with that stuff," said Basso.

"Shut up," said Pippo. "You don't know what you're talking about. Tell me, Paolo. Tell me how you can get them off it."

Paolo explained the need for reeducation, new incentives, a change in environment.

"A change in ... what?"

"A new neighborhood. Different friends."

"That's not so easy! You've done time—right? You're out, you think you're in the clear. Well, you're not. They come out and get you. If they have money, if they belong to the right gang in prison, they can escape anytime they want to. Then when they get out, they come and get you ... "

His voice broke and he pushed it back into its falsetto.

"They get you even before you come out. There was a young husband who came to the Viterbo prison. He'd stolen from a butcher to feed his family. At first, he wept every night, thinking of his wife and children, *poveretto*. But they got to him. When he came out, he was a first-class pimp, using some of his own family. That's what they do to you—unless you can separate the hard criminals from the younger ones and give them a chance to begin again, just a little chance ..."

His voice broke again. "... excuse me, I have to gargle."

Basso laughed, then lowered his voice. "It ain't easy to talk all choked up, like a girl."

Paolo thought: Poor Pippo, he's probably known someone hooked on drugs. Maybe a sister, a brother ... or a lover. Who knew? Also, Pippo himself was hooked onto a life without hope of escape—a prisoner of criminals who could not be held by prisons.

Basso turned on the radio, with the midday news: At Bologna, in a clash between police and students, a young man had been killed. Paolo heard it with a sense of personal loss.

Jesus, how sad. A young man left dead on old cobblestones in an empty piazza. What a waste. If you died fighting against fascism, fighting for liberty or for an ideal, such a death could have meaning. Yet where was the meaning of death by an accidental bullet?

They had gathered, thousands of them, in a piazza. Their struggle, they said, was against "repression." They used words like that, these young people, who had never known themselves what real repression could be.

Yet Paolo thought he understood them. They felt repressed, disbarred by their elders from a position of equality, not given a break. One million university students and another million who had graduated, floating around without jobs, trained for nothing in particular, enraged at the society that had spawned them and the political parties whose promises had not been kept—enraged even at the Communist party which they felt had betrayed them by making common cause with the government. Nothing left to believe in, except a vague, romanticized cult of revolution.

Some painted their faces and called themselves Metropolitan Indians, which was a way of saying, "Let me live!"—motors working beautifully, yet in reverse. Others carried guns, which was wrong. Yet for many, this was less to injure or to kill than to finally be heard by the deaf.

Who was at fault for this lack of concern of one generation for another, one class for another? Was it the unions? There was divorce in Italy now, but you couldn't fire a worker. Or even move him. His immobility was sacrosanct. So you didn't expand. You sat on what you had. You held on, while labor costs went skyrocketing, while there was only a slight rise in France and it remained level in West Germany. At this rate, Italy would price itself out of the Common Market, and every other market as well.

Of course, it wasn't just the unions. Was it industry, whose resistance to the most necessary reforms had all too often driven the unions to these expedients? Was it the politicians, who accepted bribes, protected the Mafia, and disgraced their office for personal gain? Were these miserable men themselves the victims of an earlier corruption, inheritors of a Fascist wasteland, with no vision of the honesty and community needed to make democracy work?

Their crime was not caring for anyone except themselves, their political parties, their children, their wives, their mistresses, their dogs. They were criminally deaf, and on them hung the tragedy of Italy today.

He heard Pippo returning and wondered where he belonged. He was lost, too—even more than the Italian youth, because they were still searching. They went on meeting in cobblestoned piazzas, getting shot at and even killed, seeking some answer to their hopes, even though no one had yet appeared whom they could trust.

Prisoners of crime like Pippo had given up. Without hope, they no longer sought to escape. Nothing could change the course of their lives. Or could it? Certainly, no one lived without some shred of hope. You fastened onto little things. You reached out for stardust or cobwebs. Or you stared at a blade of grass.

Pippo certainly had something or someone he cared for. If one could reach that, perhaps even he could be helped.

"Pippo, about the drugs. Was it someone close to you? Maybe in your family?"

"What family? I don't even know who my father was...or my mother." He swore and then fell silent.

OUTSIDE: It was a day of chaos—beginning with a call to Anna from Padre Salvatore. Unaware of having driven away the kidnappers, he had remained faithful to their first words: "We will call you at any hour with instructions on what to do. Don't fail to be there. It's a matter of life and death for Paolo."

So the old priest had sat up all night, next to a dormitory phone in a hallway, waiting for the call to save Paolo. Now in the second day, he was falling asleep. Could he take off for a couple of hours, for prayer in the chapel and a little snooze?

Anna dressed quickly and went to see Renzo and his wife. There were, she explained, too many different calls being made; they all had to be centered on one secret phone with someone they could trust. It could mean everything—even Paolo's life. It was a great deal to ask of anyone, but would they accept the bandits' phone calls?

Renzo—the actual name is withheld to preserve anonymity—did not hesitate: "Of course, Anna, we'll do whatever is needed of us."

Leaving them, she called Gigi from a subway station—dialing a special number he had given her for that morning: a broker's office where he was buying surplus Dutch butter through the Common Market. Convinced their phones were tapped by Delfino, they now made important calls from public phones to preselected numbers. They also spoke in simple code. Anna, for example, told Gigi that she had found a "harbor" (safe contact point) for Paolo's "friends" (the bandits) and would explain it to him that night at "the table" (Manzoni's law office). Also, Delfino was referred to as "the aquatic mammal."

While Anna was at Renzo's, a call came to Prisco's office, even though he was supposed to be "burnt out." The lawyer was not in—or not available—and the bandits spoke into the message machine. Their first and only attempt to contact Prisco was rough in language and overblown in manner.

They said Paolo was ill. He suffered from allergies. He needed help badly. The family had to hurry up and pay for him before it was too late. Otherwise, they'd send them an ear or a finger.

Prisco was one of the few officers of the famed Alpine Giulia Division to have survived their tragic retreat in World War II—staggering homeward from the Russian Front over the frozen bodies of his comrades.

"Sons of bitches," he said, his gray eyes looking at the tape. "Who can stop this? It's an industry with no union employees, no labor rules, no strikes, no absenteeism, no unemployment insurance—not even burial fees. It's all net profit.

"We have to get behind them ... to the politicians and men who are making millions out of this. I'm not saying exactly that the Mafia is sitting in our Parliament ... but Parliament hasn't been able to get rid of them. You figure it out."

THAT EVENING, Manzoni told Gigi and Anna that he had received a call from the captors, saying they'd left a message with Prisco. So he had called Prisco and learned the bandits had made some violent threats.

The lawyer saw a motive behind both calls. Prisco's name had figured in the papers as the Lazzaronis' contact man. As a result, the bandits knew his phone was tapped by Delfino.

"So in phoning Prisco, they are telling Major Delfino and also telling us, that Prisco is finished as a contact. It's their way of pressuring us to find another contact—and quickly."

"I've found one," Anna said. "But I don't know how to tell them, without being overheard by Delfino."

THE FIRST CALL to Renzo, using the number Paolo had given them, came after midnight. It awakened the maid who explained the Signore was away for the weekend.

"Get them, Signorina, get them fast. It's a matter of life and death."

Then a click. Terrified, the girl phoned Renzo and his wife at their weekend retreat. Shortly before 2 A.M., Anna was awakened by the phone next to her bed.

She could hear pay tokens falling and knew it was a long-distance call from a public phone—then the voice of Renzo's wife.

"Darling, we're returning tomorrow. My husband has had an urgent business call. I thought you'd like to know."

"Thank you, oh, God, thank you ..." murmured Anna.

WHEN MAJOR DELFINO learned about Don Salvatore—through intercepting the phones of Pia and Anna—he knew why there had been no registered calls from the bandits the day before. Paolo had given them a priest. Not a bad idea. Very good, in fact. But this priest sounded like a dummy. His yelling at the bandits must have been a riot—an Italian comedy with Toto and the original gang that couldn't shoot straight.

Delfino smiled, imagining the scene. He was seated before his desk at the carabiniere command post, waiting for a return call from a squad car that had picked up two men in a stolen car.

He could see the old priest in worn sandals and brown Franciscan robes, yelling into the phone, trying to instruct the bandits on human rights. No wonder they had been so rough and angry in later calls. It had made them look foolish. That was dangerous because the criminal mind cannot take ridicule. You had to study their behavior and thought patterns to get the picture.

First of all, the criminal is perpetually angry, even when he's drinking an espresso. Next, he has an insecure overinflated pride, and a mind consumed by fears—large and small, real and imagined. Ridicule and laughter can unseat such minds, plunging their superegos down to a flat zero state. When that occurs, criminals become highly irrational and dangerous. They imagine offense and see nonexistent dangers.

In such moments, they strike out at anything, and it is then that kidnap victims run their greatest risk of being killed.

Lazzaroni's captors must have been especially rough on him when they came back from the priest. If he was smart, Lazzaroni would have taken it and not talked back....

The shortwave set behind Delfino crackled, and his call came from a brigadier in a squad car. The two men caught stealing an Alfa Romeo both came from the south—one from Sicily, the other Calabria.

"Where in Calabria?" asked Delfino.

"Platì, Signor Maggiore."

Platì—his hometown. *Madonna,* another one. Another crook from Calabria. Another name in the papers to make people think that Calabria was a breeding ground for gangsters. It wasn't true. There were hundreds of thousands of honest, hard-working Calabrians. They had immigrated all over the world—to Argentina, to Austria, and even to Pennsylvania in the U.S.A. Honest people. But a few crooks were giving the place a terrible name.

What made one man go one way—into crime—while another led an honest life? Delfino had seen it happen so often, he felt he knew. Man was born good and he was made bad by society, by his environment. Top Mafia chiefs sent their sons to universities, to the best schools, expecting them to lead decent lives—only to find them joining the mob. They chose it because, for them, it was the only life that was a challenge, that gave the excitement of growth—and power. Sometimes it was pathetic. Like the fourth-year medical student who cut off the ear of a classmate being held for ransom. To change it, you had to change society. That meant better men in government and better magistrates—unafraid of threats, untempted by bribes ...

"Signor Maggiore?"

"Yes?"

"There's something about these two guys ... the way they took the car and how they're talking. Makes me think it was for a kidnapping."

"Bring them in," ordered Delfino. "Don't let them know what you suspect."

SATURDAY
The 6th Day

PAOLO AWOKE and felt his heart skip a beat. Oh, Jesus, not now. Not another attack of arrhythmia. He took some deep breaths, and heard his pounding heart: *boom-buh, boom-buh* ...

No, thank God. Not this time. When it happened, you knew it. It was like someone strangling your heart while it beat wildly, trying to get free.

Yet he had to get ready for it. If it happened in this place, he would need to take the medicine immediately. What was the name of the drug? It had a strange name. Anna knew it. He tried to recall it but could not.

His mind drifted away to his family. What was Anna doing? It must be very hard for her now. And the children? Did they know? He would have to tell them someday. Maybe he should write a letter to them and keep it until they were old enough to understand. He could explain that this was like life itself, or perhaps like Italy today. You held on to your beliefs, your dreams, your faith, even though you were in the dark. Only then, when you couldn't see, was there any real test of your strength, your manhood. You measured it against a growing awareness of being alone in the world—as he was now, bound and blinded in an airless room. Yes ... if he survived, he would try and tell it to his children.

They would understand it when they were older, when it began to happen to them—when they realized it was a central condition of life and no one, no matter how clean, could change it or make the crossing to your shore. It happened to everyone, but perhaps men felt it more keenly, more intensely because they did not live with children growing within them, eventually nourishing them from their own bodies.

The special loneliness of man lay there. He could never talk about it with a woman without losing something that was special and binding between them. Nor could he speak of his fear of failure, or his periodic need to feel himself as the center of the universe. He had to feel that to be a man. Without it, he lost a central hardness, a sense of personal worth and power—and without it, he could not perform as a man.

All of this he would write in a letter for his children to read many years from now. It would explain much to them—and to Anna, too, if she opened herself to how it related to their own lives.

OUTSIDE: Renzo was back at his apartment at 2 P.M. Anna came over and one hour later there was a call—the first direct contact with Renzo by Paolo's captors.

The Caller asked if Renzo was ready to handle all future calls. Renzo said he was. Prompted by Anna, he asked the answer to the last question from Paolo. The Caller gave it and Renzo had a new question: What was the name of the little girl Paolo and Anna had known and liked very much last summer during their holiday?

Renzo then explained he worked during the day so no calls should come before 10 P.M. How was Paolo? The Caller said he was fine, they'd call again later—but they'd also continue to make cover calls to Manzoni. This, however, was to be the real contact.

That evening, the Anna-Gigi-Manzoni triumvirate decided there had been too many calls—including a registration heard by office girls—using the same password. Besides, there might be another gang, or a splinter group within this gang, trying to grab off the ransom money. So now that Renzo's line was secure, they had to make sure they were dealing with the real captors ... and to know also that Paolo was all right.

Anna left for Renzo's apartment to tell him of their decision. Driving there, she thought about a question that had troubled her all day: How did it happen that she and Paolo had both selected Renzo? They had many other friends. Yet, independently, they had both chosen the same man. Why?

It had to be because they were so close, almost the same person, with nothing separating them—not even a doubt or a hidden fear. She knew how Paolo felt and thought—clear to the center of his soul—as he knew how she felt. It had been that way from the beginning because she had insisted upon it.

Only yesterday, while waiting for Gigi, she had talked about it with his wife, Pucci, who was wondering why one marriage out of every three crumbled? Why did the other two hold together? Anna told her she could speak only for herself and Paolo, but ... well, love was like a house. If you didn't take care of it, it fell apart. If you had money, it helped. If you worked or had separate interests to share and grow together, it also helped. But talking was most important.

"Talking about what?" Pucci asked.

"About what's inside," Anna replied. "When I met Paolo, I felt immediately a need to have in him an alter ego. I didn't want mysteries of any sort between us. I wanted to be able to tell him whatever came into my head, no matter what. He has to be another me, another self of me ... a total ongoing confession of self. And I hope I'm that way for him."

"I think it's a question of identity," said Pucci. "If you are prevented from being yourself, you suffer and it goes badly."

Anna nodded. "Or else, you help the other to find his identity. We had trouble at first because Paolo had been a bachelor so long, and he has a way of pushing things aside. He can fight with someone, then, after half a day, talk to them as though nothing had happened. I can't do that. I told him if there's anything that seems unjust or unfair, I want it put on the table, even if it means a fight."

"Not always," said Pucci. "You'll find there's some things you can't put on the table—ever."

Anna studied her sister-in-law, sitting on a sofa in her home. Pucci was wise in many ways. What was she trying to tell her? Something about Paolo she didn't know?

"No," she said. "I think you must discuss it, no matter what—a flirt, maybe, or a temper tantrum. You have to explain your feelings, otherwise you lose touch."

"I'm saying something else," replied Pucci. "If you're really strong and sure of your love, you don't have to constantly add things up, checking them out on a table. You can be free about it ... not so tight."

"Meaning what?"

"To stand together, you have to be able to stand alone."

What was Pucci saying? To get ready to live without Paolo? Anna shuddered, then said no more as others entered the room.

ANNA FOUND RENZO at dinner with his wife, and she joined them for coffee while waiting for a call from the bandits. Time passed slowly and they began the game of Monopoly. Finally, at 10 P.M., the phone rang. Renzo took it and nodded to Anna that it was the bandit Caller. Following her instructions, he explained that they wanted a new password, because the old one was known to too many people—priests, secretaries, and others—and also because there seemed to be other people trying to get into the act.

"Other people? Who are they?" asked the Caller, alarmed.

"It's just our impression," explained Renzo. "So ask Paolo the name of the black guide he and Anna used on their honeymoon in Uganda. That can be our password from now on ... all right?"

"What other people are calling you?"

"We don't know ... strange calls."

"The police?"

Renzo and Anna were suddenly alarmed. If the bandits thought this phone was tapped, they would hang up.

"No, not the police," said Renzo, trying to reassure them. "It's somebody else we don't know, and they called the family. They didn't call here. Nobody's called here, except you."

"The money. You got it?"

"And one other thing, if you don't mind. We'd like to have a photo of Paolo."

"The money, I said."

"We're getting it. You get the photo and we'll meet your request as best we can."

AT THE CARABINIERI COMMAND, the two car thieves told a similar story: They had met a man at a bar who gave them 5,000 lire to drive his car to the train station, park it, and wait for him at the newsstand. They had accepted his money and started off—only to be arrested. It was a dirty trick. They ought to arrest the crook who got them into this mess.

The owner of the car turned out to be an electronics engineer who, at the moment his car was stolen, was in bed with his mistress. Not wanting his wife to know about it, the engineer preferred to drop all charges.

Delfino requested that the responsible magistrate order the two men to be held over, pending a check on their identity, documents, and police records.

"Keep them apart," he asked. "Don't let them even see each other from a distance. After two days, they won't know what the other one might have said."

Throughout the day, he had hoped for some word from Antonio—hope against hope. Maybe they had not caught him. Maybe he'd gotten away and was in hiding.

He had also looked for some evidence of calls to the Lazzaronis—but nothing appeared. Were they stumped for their next move? Or had those resourceful Lazzaronis managed, at last, to find a safe phone?

He studied the day's report: Manzoni off to dinner with friends. Gigi Lazzaroni, ditto. Well, it was Saturday night.

But during the day ... earlier in the day, Anna had paid a brief visit to a friend in an apartment building near Piazza Brescia. Who? This was something new.

SUNDAY
The 7th Day

E WAS BACK in Amazonia, retracing a dramatic and dangerous journey. The Indios had revolted, killing three whites, and he was working his way through the brush toward an area where there was less chance of being captured.

"Hey, Paolo, get up and make yourself beautiful."

It was Pippo. He obeyed, fighting off any hope that he was being freed. They never told him how it was going and he never asked. Either way, it would disturb him emotionally. It was better to avoid any psychological setbacks. Or to ask for favors. He had never said: "I can't use a pot, I want a toilet." That would create a debt—if there was a toilet to be had.

Pippo sat him down in the chair. They placed something over his eye bandages.

"What's that?"

"Eyeglasses. Take this—it's a newspaper. Hold it up, like this, so we can see the date. Now don't move."

He heard a click, and Pippo said he could relax. They had taken a Polaroid photo to send to his wife.

"She wants to see how you are."

"I stink. I must look awful. My beard feels like a mop. I can't stand the smell. How can you stand it, Pippo?"

"I used to take care of chickens. They stink worse than anything, even hogs."

Paolo gave the newspaper back to Pippo.

"What paper is it?"

"Il Giorno."

"What are the headlines?"

"Madonna mia!" exclaimed Pippo. "Vallanzasca got twenty-one years and four months."

The famous bandit had committed a series of spectacular crimes—including kidnapping a young girl, Emanuela Trapani, and forcing her, among other things, to make his own bed and lay out his silk pajamas.

"The poor bastard," said Pippo. "There's a picture of his mother kissing him. At least he's got a mother."

After a moment, Pippo continued: "Why'd the bastards have to put four months on top of twenty-one years?"

"What else is there?" asked Paolo.

"It says there's a new Europe now and the young people are getting a better deal ... but that's a lot of horseshit. If it were true, there wouldn't be poor bastards like Vallanzasca. You agree, Paolo?"

"Maybe you're right, Pippo."

Maybe, too, he had been right. Obviously, Pippo was capable of caring. If one could find the heart of it, perhaps something could be done.

OUTSIDE: During the night, a heavily armed carabiniere patrol left Saronno, heading for a small village near Lake Como. Their mission: Seize and occupy a farmhouse in which Paolo Lazzaroni was believed to be held captive.

No one knew what to expect. No carabinieri unit had ever moved with such a mixed bag of superstition and military intelligence. The first element came from France. Upon learning of the kidnapping, the Lazzaroni representative in Paris had consulted a famous French clairvoyant who declared that Paolo was held in or near a village close to Lake Como. At the same time, the chef at the Lazzaroni Grill—a combined restaurant and gift center near the factory—told Gigi he possessed infallible vision in locating missing objects and persons. Dangling a pendulum over a map with Paolo's photo, he had come up with the same village cited by the French clairvoyant.

Gigi didn't believe in such matters. He knew Anna did, however, and took the reports of the two clairvoyants to the carabinieri command at Saronno. He did not tell Anna. He wanted to avoid false hopes or fear that Paolo might be killed in gunfire by the liberating police.

The carabinieri looked at the two reports without knowing what to do about them. No one had ever mounted a military operation on the basis of a swinging pendulum. On the other hand, how could a famous clairvoyant in Paris and a Lazzaroni cook in Italy both point to the same village without speaking to one another?

Careful inquiries were made in the area. It was discovered that, indeed, there had been some mysterious movement around a farmhouse close to the village. Immediately, the Saronno command moved with decision. A patrol was formed with orders to move in before dawn and disarm all occupants before they could put up resistance or start a gun battle.

The assault went off on schedule and the patrol seized the farmhouse—finding five chickens, a pair of doves, an empty pig pen ... but no other occupants. No one was wounded in the operation, except one man who, on creeping up Indian style, fell off a wall and sprained his shoulder.

THE PHONE RANG at 7 P.M. Anna stood next to Renzo as he answered it—and heard the new password.

"Justus," said the Caller.

It was the closest his Italian tongue could get to "Justice." In this way, a Uganda tribesman, baptized into the Christian faith by passing missionaries, was resurrected again in Milan, his name modified still further on the lips of the underworld and a few respectable citizens collaborating with criminals in order to save the life of one man.

"Go ahead," Renzo said.

There was a phone booth on a street corner near Piazza Brescia, where Renzo lived. They would find a photo of Paolo there—under the phone box. They could expect another call within the hour.

Anna drove rapidly to the street corner. Approaching the phone booth, she saw someone leaving it. Oh, Signore, did Delfino know? Inside, pretending to make a call, she found an envelope attached by adhesive tape to the bottom of the phone box.

Unable to wait, she tore it open. Paolo was seated in a chair, wearing dark glasses and smiling. Behind the glasses there was a bandage, and a tape wound around his head. He couldn't see! He was blinded! The glasses were to make him appear less gruesome. He held a copy of *Il Giorno* in front of him, with "Justus" hand-printed across the front page. His head poked over the top of the sheet, and he was smiling, as though it were all a joke.

She felt her knees giving way, and she held on to the phone box.

That face and that smile—it was Paolo trying to tell her: "Don't worry, my love, I'm all right. Look, you can see me. Just hold on, like I am...."

Turning it over, she saw his name scrawled out as though written without vision: *Paolo Lazzaroni*. The *n* was too high and the *o* was not closed. Beneath it was another series of letters forming two words: *Nossi be*—the name of their honeymoon isle, the island of intermingling waters with the scent of flowers. Their paradise had been scribbled out on the back of a Polaroid photo, while he was smiling for her, telling her to take courage ... hold on, my love.

She was going to faint and she left the booth, running toward her car. Seated behind the wheel, she began to cry, saying over and over, "Oh, Paolo, I'll do it, I'll hold on ... I'll not fail you." The streets were blurred by tears.

Anna's bittersweet victory soon tumbled into disaster. After she returned, Renzo received a second call.

"Got what you wanted?"

"Yes, thank you."

"Is the wife happy?"

"Yes. Tell her husband that she loves his smile and she thinks he's *molto bravo.*"

"Have you got the stuff ready?"

"Stuff" meant money. But 3 billion lire of it was astronomical—far beyond the reach of any Lazzaroni.

"We're getting it together, as much as we can."

"How much you got?"

A rule of this game was to open with a low bid. Renzo did just that.

"One hundred fifty million."

That was about $170,000. He heard a scraping sound, as though the phone was once more passing over a beard, to be shared with another listener—probably the gang leader.

"Only one-fifty?"

Again a shuffling across a beard.

"All right, if you want to play that way. We'll talk to you again at Ferragosto ... "—then a click.

Ferragosto? The Italian mid-August holiday was six months away! Paolo would never survive that long! Even his smile told you that. If they meant what they said, everything was lost.

DELFINO KNEW something was up upon learning from a patrol car that Anna had gone back to the same apartment of the day before. It wasn't for dinner, however, because shortly after 7 P.M. she came out and drove to a phone booth. Emerging, she had an envelope in her hand. It was the same old trick. Using phone booths for drop points. After that, she had returned to the same building.

So it was definite: They had found their contact; they had their safe phone. It had to be in that apartment house. But which apartment? He couldn't have her followed inside the building or ask the doorman. The doorman would rat at the first chance. They all ratted.

No, he'd have to obtain authorization to monitor every phone in the building until he found the right one. Also, from the city registry, he'd get a list of every occupant, their ages and profession. It would eliminate many and indicate, among the few remaining, that friend or relative who was the Lazzaroni's secret link with the bandits.

There was time. The message left in the phone booth was probably a letter from Paolo—proof they really had him. It wasn't instructions for paying the ransom. So far, the Lazzaronis hadn't even tried to draw out their money.

AT HOME THAT EVENING, Delfino surprised his wife with travel brochures for Greece and Morocco. He spread them out on the living-room table and told her to take her choice.

"What'll it be? The wonders of Greece or the marvels of Morocco."

"Franco! Really?"

He nodded, feeling pleasure at her happiness. They were going to see the world, thanks to the Mafia. He couldn't go home on vacation without risk to his family. So they were going abroad and Carla was happy—the kids, too.

Drawn by their mother's cries of joy, Stefania and Andrea came running into the room. Seeing the brochures, they quickly took their choice.

"Greece!" cried Stefania. "We're going to study it in history class!"

"Morocco!" yelled Andrea. "Sheiks with big swords on horses!"

Carla happily kissed her husband on his nose. He pressed her thigh and imagined them in a hotel by the sea.

"In Morocco," she said. "I could get some unusual cloth for curtains—maybe with a gold thread."

"That settles it," he said, glancing at one of their bare windows.

When they had moved into the apartment, built in the Fascist era with high ceilings and windows, Carla had found their curtains were too short and had refused to buy new ones. They had moved eight times in fourteen years and she was fed up. Until they had a place with normal windows, or until they stopped drifting like gypsies, the windows could go bare. But take her to Morocco and everything was solved. The wonders of this trip were infinite: Tropical love, sheiks with flashing swords, golden curtains....

The phone rang and Carla answered it.

"Somebody named Antonio."

"Hang up," he told her. "I'll take it in the kitchen."

When he picked it up, the carabiniere at the switchboard repeated the message.

"Signor Maggiore, the caller says it's from Antonio."

"Okay. Record it and trace it. Put him on."

There was a pause—then the call came through.

"Maggiore Delfino?"

It was a woman.

"Yes?"

"I'm the wife of Antonio."

It was a trap. Antonio's wife knew nothing about the arrangement. They had caught Antonio and forced him to talk, and now were using this woman as his wife to get more information.

"Antonio who? I don't know what you're talking about."

"They said you would."

"Who did?"

"This man called on the phone and said you would know where Antonio is. He hasn't come home since Tuesday, and now it's Sunday and I don't know where he is. I wait by the phone, and he never calls. But the man said you would know."

"Did he say who he was?"

"No, he only said I should ask you, and he gave me the number to call."

"What else did he say?"

"He said Antonio was going on a long trip and you would know."

"Nothing more?"

"No, Signor Maggiore. Did you arrest my Antonio?"

It was the wife all right. But maybe they were forcing her to talk.

"I don't know your husband. I haven't seen him or arrested him. I'm sorry."

"Why did they tell me to ask you? Please help me, please...."

She was sobbing now. They had two children, almost the same ages as Andrea and Stefania. Antonio had carried a photo of them in his wallet—the two kids and Antonio with his wife, all of them in swimming suits, squinting into the sun. The girl was smiling, and the boy had his arms crossed on his chest to make the muscles bigger. Antonio held his wife proudly, as though they were on a honeymoon.

"I'm frightened, Signor Maggiore. If you don't have Antonio, then someone else has him, and maybe they're going to kill him. He's innocent, isn't he? He's a good man, isn't he?"

The photo had a bent edge. When Antonio took it out of his wallet, he would try to straighten it before showing it to you.

"I don't know him, Signora. But I'm sure he's a very good man."

"What can I do? Where can I go to find him?"

"I don't know. If we hear of anything, we'll let you know."

He asked for her address and phone number. It was Antonio's. Perhaps she was not being forced to make the call. Perhaps it was as she had said it. But he could never let her know. If there was one chance in a thousand for Antonio to still be alive, this might blow it.

In the living room, he found Carla reading the Morocco travel brochure to the children. She stopped and they all stared at him.

"Is everything all right, Franco?"

"Yes."

"Who's Antonio?"

"Nobody."

He looked at the bare window—black against the dark night. In Morocco there would be bright stars. They would be low in the sky, and Carla would reach up to touch them. Maybe somewhere in this world Antonio could see them, too.

MONDAY
The 8th Day

WAKING UP, he heard them shouting at each other. He couldn't make out the words, but the tone was violent. Then a door slammed—followed by silence.

Pippo brought in breakfast but didn't stay to talk. Something was wrong. It couldn't be that the family was trying to outsmart them. Not Anna. She'd be playing it straight. It had to be money. They were asking too much. Some sum beyond all reason.

It occurred to Paolo that the next move was his. Anna needed his help. He would talk to Bogey. Pippo and Basso were only custodians—or better, cellmates. Bogey was the man.

He would tell him many things about Italy today, saying it in simple words so Bogey would understand. It wasn't only the life of one Lazzaroni. It wasn't only their company. It was the whole country—and where it was heading.

Italy was becoming a nation of bankrupt capitalism. Most of the major industrial firms were heading for bankruptcy. Their sales were big, but their overhead ate up their profits and piled up more debt. Alfa-Sud managed to lose $4,000 on every car it sold. Italsider, the steel company, had $2.5 billion sales in the last report—but lost $147 million. So it went with many others.

Many of these companies were being saved from bankruptcy

only by bailouts from the government, which itself was near bankruptcy. The budget deficit last year was $12 billion—double that if calculated realistically. Foreign debts were $17 billion. Private funds were fleeing the country. Everyone was buying land elsewhere, especially apartments and farmland in the United States.

Italy's economic backbone was not in these large companies. It was in the small- and medium-sized industries, concentrated mainly in Lombardy, like the Lazzaronis. There were 18,000 of them—only 20 percent of the Italian total. Yet they produced 40 percent of its GNP.

Two giants, Motta and Alemagna, had tried for years to buy them out, but his father had refused. Now both those firms faced bankruptcy, while Lazzaroni continued to survive. How? By hard work, and by staying with it—using the latest in production and marketing techniques. To do this, however, they had to invest everything in the firm.

He and his father and his brother Gigi were not sending money abroad. They did not own apartments in the Olympic Tower on Fifth Avenue in New York. They were staying home. Like most Italians, they believed in their nation, and nothing—nothing, not Eurocommunism or the Red Brigades or whatever else you could dream up—would prevail against them. That was why they couldn't pay the kind of ransom the gang had in mind.

Someone entered the room, slow and heavy: Bogey himself.

"If your family thinks we're going to let you go for a plate of spaghetti, they're crazy. You can lie here and rot for a year, until they get some damn sense in their heads."

"I've been hoping you'd come," said Paolo. "I want to explain why we have no cash. It's all in the factory—in machines and labor and stocks of cookies in the warehouse."

"Fuck your cookies," said Bogey. "We want dough ... real dough."

OUTSIDE: Anna waited all evening at Renzo's. There were no calls, other than her usual evening talk with the children. They seemed happy and well. Luca had skied on the big slope without permission and had had a bad spill. But he was without injury and apparently much wiser. Marco had found a little girl he liked and was less of a nuisance to his brother.

Shortly after midnight, she went home. She lay on Paolo's side of the bed and wondered what would happen to them. No calls today. Maybe they wouldn't call tomorrow or next week—or for a month. Paolo would never be able to endure that....

She looked at the golden figures of two angels hanging on the wall at the foot of the bed. Yes, this was something more than a pending tragedy. It was a religious experience. She had always assumed that she understood the words of the Scripture. But not until now did she really feel them deep within her. She was living them every moment. It was that which gave her the strength to go on, day and night, without rest.

In bed, she thought: We think we believe in the Church, but it's our lips that are moving, not our hearts. It's true, as Jesus said: "If you ask the Lord, my Father, something in my name, it will be given unto you...."

She spoke out loud, toward the two angels, saying: *"Signore,* I ask this not for me, not for my merits because I'm probably the lowest being on earth. I ask it in your name for your Son...."

It seemed to her when she asked it that way—with all her being, all her soul—that it was really happening. She felt certain that she was being heard.

She began to pray again, "I ask it, O Lord, not for me, but for your Son...."

At that moment, a small miracle was given to her—sleep.

MAJOR DELFINO'S REPORT showed her going to the same apartment house again. All the lines in the building had been tapped. But for the second straight day, no calls from the bandits— not on the cover-up lines, not on the real one, whichever one it was.

He'd received a list of all the occupants and been able to eliminate half of them—leaving six possibilities. Of these, another three would probably be eliminated. But until he had a call, it would remain a bucket of clams.

Were these subtle upper-class Lazzaronis trying to trick him—

using Anna as a decoy while they set up a safe line elsewhere? No, that would be too Machiavellian, even for them. They probably didn't realize they would be tailed as well as tapped.

Did Anna have a lover? No, she wasn't the type. The contact phone was in that building. *Pazienza.* Sooner or later, the bandits would have to make that call.

In late afternoon, Major Delfino received a report which appeared to link the Lazzaroni bandits to another kidnapping. A computer in Turin had determined that the voiceprints of the Caller in the Lazzaroni case were identical to those of someone who had made calls in another case where the ransom had been paid, but the victim had not yet been returned.

This was not especially good news for the Lazzaronis. It was, however, most important for Delfino. Two suspects in the same kidnap case were on Delfino's list of twenty-nine names, believed to form part of a large kidnap network. So two kidnappings, at least, had been done by one group—perhaps more.

Was it all controlled by one gang, united in one overall Kidnap Inc.? If so, it meant that an entry into one operation—identifying the men running it—would lead to others. *Madonna!* The mass arrest of the entire group might break the back of the organized kidnappings in Milan—at least for a time, until a new one began. It would enable them to liberate Paolo Lazzaroni without payment of ransom, along with three or four others—perhaps more if they were still alive.

This was probably the same gang that had seized Antonio. Perhaps they were also making threatening phone calls to investigating magistrates like Pomarici in Milan. Anyone seriously opposing the Mafia was threatened—judges, lawyers, attorney generals, the police, carabinieri, members of Parliament. Anybody who got in their way could expect a warning.

You had to know how to read Mafia warnings and also know when they became serious. Some were meant simply to frighten, like barking dogs. Others were a real threat, and still others had the finality of a death sentence. It depended upon how dangerous you were. If you knew their structure and operational command, especially what they intended to do in the future, you were considered extremely dangerous to them. When they told such people that they were already "dead," they meant it.

Was he, Francesco Delfino, in that category? What had Antonio told them? Undoubtedly, they had tortured him. A great deal depended upon what he had said under such treatment. Or— more important—what they assumed Antonio might have withheld from them.

Despite this, the threats weren't the major trouble. You could expect them. It was a rough, dirty business and this was part of it. The real problem was something else: Lack of proper support from higher authorities, both in Milan and Rome. Where the Mafia was a unified command, the forces of law in Italy were not. The various branches—carabinieri, police, public security, internal revenue— rivaled with each other and often duplicated work or failed to recognize an isolated element as being a vital link in a case elsewhere.

This lack of unity was reflected also in the cities which did not cooperate with each other and applied laws differently. Besides this, everyone lacked equipment. Turin, for example, had a voiceprint computer—not Milan. Inevitably this cost time and caused further confusion. There had to be a unified command in Milan, linked to similar commands in the other cities, to inter-change data and to track down the various gangs who had greater mobility and internal unity than those hunting them. Until that occurred—and until the government in Rome got behind all of it— they could never extinguish the Mafia, any more than a child could kill a giant octopus with a penknife.

TUESDAY
The 9th Day

PAOLO SAT in the wooden chair listening to the morning radio news. Indro Montanelli, of the right-wing paper *Il Giornale,* was examining the tortured question which crept into every conversation in Italy these days: Was the Communist party gradually taking over Italy?

Montanelli was saying he doubted it. The Communists were sharing in the government by accepting chairmanships of committees in Parliament. But not being part of the cabinet, they didn't have power to accomplish what they had promised their voters— and it was pulling the party apart. The workers felt betrayed, the unions were angry, the young people threw rocks at them. Also, Eurocommunism was nothing new. It was the same Communism, under another name. The party structure and the members remained authoritative and Marxist.

His prescription was simple: Let the Christian-Democrat government clean house, and keep the Communists out of the executive branch.

"You can't keep them out," retorted Cesare Golfari, president of the Lombardy regional government. They controlled six of Italy's twenty regions and forty-five of its ninety-four provinces and had

Communist mayors in Rome, Naples, Florence, Turin, and Bologna. Instead of trying to push them back into the ghetto, the government should involve them in specific national problems like economic development, taxes, labor costs, administrative reform. That would either transform them from a one-class party to a party for all classes, or so expose their internal contradictions on these issues that they would be discredited in the nation's eyes—with the inevitable political consequences.

Because basically, Golfari concluded, Italy remained politically mature, with a great potential, a bright future. Disorganization, violence, kidnappings? Yes, but the real issue was the emergence of violence in all industrial societies. It was a worldwide problem, a product of the age. "It's a problem we'll have to face with the Communists, allowing the people to witness and decide on their political maturity ... "

The radio was switched off and Paolo continued to think about it. Who were the Communists really? It wasn't a fixed block. It was a mass of people looking for a better deal. The party received 34 percent of the last vote, but only one voter in ten was Communist. The rest were people of all sorts, fed up with street violence, strikes, rising prices, bankrupt cities, failure to deliver mail, collect garbage, pay pensions—or even to mint money. Fed up, too, with thirty years of broken promises and corrupt rule by the Christian Democrats. So what was the alternative? There was none, except the Communist party.

That was the source of the Italian tragedy: The failure of the smaller parties to hang together—especially the Socialists. Their petty bickering and continual splitting into hysterical factions—putting the party before the people and the nation—was the gravest betrayal of the Italian promise. It left the Communists as the only real party of opposition.

Was Montanelli right? Would the party never change its stripes? Or was Golfari right in saying it would be forced to change as it came to power—or else fall apart? Either way, Italy could not continue on this course much longer.

Paolo's mind turned to Pippo. He and Pippo—two products of the age. Each, in different ways, the other's victim. How could the relationship between the Paolos and the Pippos of Italy be "managed better" in the more rational future Golfari evoked?

OUTSIDE: Driving to work, Gigi prepared for a crucial day. He had to meet with the company's fifteen key salesmen and convince them to call off their slowdown strike. An agreement could be found after Paolo was returned. For now, he wanted only their help to boost sales and shove ahead.

They would need a lot of money for Paolo's ransom. And sales were down. The company was caught in the same economic squeeze as everyone else. First, there had been the overstocking stimulated by inflation. Then, with the government's anti-inflationary measures, money got tighter. Result: A slump in consumer demand.

At the plant, Gigi found the salesmen waiting in the conference room. He made a short speech but it was hardly necessary. The group had already decided to call off the strike. They'd talk about it again after Paolo was back.

Gigi thanked them. He was profoundly moved, and he wished he could have found words to express what he felt.

In his office, there was a call from Signor Bafabio, the firm's representative in Turin.

"Dottore Luigi, I want to ask you a favor."

"What is it?"

"My son and I, for the next year, we don't want our salaries. Nothing. Absolutely nothing. You take it and use it to help pay for Paolo."

Hanging up, he felt close to tears. They'd make it. They'd pull through. And Paolo would come home. Why did you feel closest to a brother, or anyone you loved, when you were threatened with their loss?

DELFINO WENT OVER a report of calls into the building. Still nothing, even though Anna had gone there again that evening. But to which apartment? From a list of all the occupants, he saw two strong probabilities. Until the call came in, however, he couldn't be sure. There were other ways to get the information, but it wasn't worth the risk—not yet, anyway.

WEDNESDAY
The 10th Day

PAOLO'S CHANCE to escape came at mid-morning, when he heard Basso snoring. He was sitting in the wooden chair, as he did every day now, and Basso was on the other side of the room, probably in another chair—and asleep.

Pippo was also asleep. He had stood the midnight-to-6 A.M. watch, then gone to bed in another room. Basso had taken over—only to snooze off. Bogey was not there. He never came before noon.

Rapidly, Paolo calculated his chances. First, he could use his handcuffed hands to tear the tape from his eyes—but what then? If he ran for it, the front door would be locked. The window? He remembered being brought up the stairs. The window, if there was one, would be at least two stories high.

If he yelled out the window for help, they would certainly kill him. They had made that clear the first day when they had switched the handcuffs to the front: "If you lift off your tape and see us, we'll kill you. If you happen to see us for any reason, we'll kill you. Get that into your head and never forget it."

That left only one possibility. Take off the tape, grab Basso's submachine gun and kill him. Then run into Pippo's room and kill him. Find the keys on one of them and walk out.

It depended on finding a gun in the instant he removed the

tape. Basso probably had one in his lap or leaning against his chair. You could hear him when he put it down, the gun butt hitting the floor with a thud. In fact, he had at least two guns, because on the second day he had stuck a muzzle into Paolo's ribs and said, "This is a German machine gun." Then he had stuck him from the other side, saying: "This is an Italian one, feel the difference?" Basso had laughed at that. It was his idea of educating the blind.

So the gun was there. He only had to grab it fast. The whole thing wouldn't take more than a minute. Three seconds to pull off the tape. Two seconds to grab Basso's gun. One shot in the head. Then run into Pippo's room and—

Santo Cielo, what was he thinking of? How could he kill Pippo asleep, or sitting up in the bed, with no time to know anything before the bullets cut down his frail body? Because he was frail, a little man. Even though he had never seen him, Paolo sensed him that way. That was Pippo, who cooked him his food and brought him his tray, saying, "O.K., Paolo, the fruit is on the right, the beer's on the left, and I hope the veal isn't too tough today." Pippo, who'd asked about how to help drug addicts. Pippo, who'd never known the love of a father or mother. Pippo, with the squeezed-up tiny voice....

His heart was beating wildly. He was sweating. It was insane to think this way. Or was he being a coward? He had to be sure. He had to think of his own life, of Anna, of his sons. If he didn't take this chance, he might never see them again. Perhaps these men were allowing him to live merely to answer Anna's questions. And then, when they obtained the money—*addio.*

Yet now, before they could do that, he had this chance. Just kill them quickly and run out without looking back. But no—he'd see them anyway: A man in a chair with the top of his head blown off. Another one twisted about in sheets red with blood, his eyes open with terror even in death. He'd see it all in an instant that would last a lifetime. No matter what he did, it would stay with him. He'd never be able to run away from it. Nor from the sounds of the voices. Maybe Pippo would speak in his normal voice, sitting upright in bed, small hands covering his bare chest as he begged for his life: "Paolo!...Please don't ... oh, God, PaoloooOOHH!"

He dropped his head on his chest and began to take deep breaths. He breathed in harmony with Basso's snoring, until, with one loud snort, Basso woke himself up. Paolo heard a sound like the butt end of a gun hitting the floor.

Fearing that Basso might suspect him of having taken a peek at him from under the bandages, he pretended to wake up with a start.

"What's up?" he cried. "What's going on?"

"What the hell do you think is going on?" Basso snarled, to cover his confusion.

"Oh, it's you. Sorry. Guess I fell asleep."

OUTSIDE: The press conference appeared to be a brilliant idea. The kidnappers had not called for three days. Apparently, they had meant it when they said they would not call again until *Ferragosto.* So something had to be done to break the deadlock.

After the first big spreads, the papers had stayed off the case—at Manzoni's request—on the assumption that publicity whetted the kidnappers' appetite for higher ransom. But, Gigi argued, maybe that was true only of the usual kind of publicity. What if they opened their gates—their books, in a manner of speaking—to the press?

Let the reporters see for themselves the situation the Lazzaronis were in, unable to raise the kind of money the kidnappers wanted because they were a medium-sized concern that plowed profits back into production so as to survive against domestic odds and foreign competition—even against the British biscuit industry, with its traditional markets around the world. Couldn't the press be counted on to write heartfelt stories about this intrepid, family-owned Italian enterprise threatened with being sunk, along with its little trademark of a boat, the *Esportazione,* by the exorbitant demands of a gang of crooks?

The bandits were putting psychological pressure on the Lazzaronis. Well, this would put some psychological pressure on them. The workers were worried about rumors of a pay cut to help raise the ransom money. Let them speak their fears. Let them say whatever they wanted to. It could only help.

The press turnout was large. The group was escorted to the factory floor, past the production lines being fed their correct portions of flour, sugar, butter, and other ingredients from a master computer, on to a glass-enclosed room, for a session with representatives of management and labor—including twelve young women wearing white work gowns and white caps.

Beyond the young women, through the glass partition, one could see five long production lines of the factory moving to accept from a master computer the correct proportions of flour (3,500 tons a year), sugar (1,800 tons), butter (240 tons). Combined with other ingredients, it was blended, rolled, stamped, and then baked on slow-moving belts passing through tunnel ovens—all of it emerging into 41 million boxes (using 200 tons of aluminum foil) to finally go out to the four corners of the world for gross sales of $25 million.

Two men and a woman representing the union were seated at a table in front of the young women. Nicolo de Benedictis, the union spokesman, sat in the middle. Unlike all the others in white factory gowns, he wore a dark blue T-shirt. He was lean, ruggedly handsome, and had the down-plunging Fu Manchu mustache one sees in spaghetti Westerns.

De Benedictis read from a prepared script, stating the employees were astonished and even frightened by the kidnapping. They hoped nothing they said today would compromise Paolo's safe return. But if the family didn't have enough money for the ransom, it would be a great wrong to allow this to jeopardize employees' paychecks.

The newsmen exchanged surprised glances. They had expected to hear little more than a pro-company talk from a selected group of factory workers. Gigi had not done that, wanting the union to select its own representatives. De Benedictis—a Marxist, with little intention of deviating from an "objective" line—continued to give the union position:

"Why should workers pay for the government's failure to prevent this kind of crime? If we helped pay for the ransom, we'd create a precedent and jeopardize workers in other plants. That could lead to the kidnapping of workers as well as bosses."

Other employees spoke up. All expressed sympathy for Paolo

and the Lazzaroni family. But they were afraid. They were afraid this might even put them out of work. Some of them said they were ready to march on the prefect of police and demand that he do something about these crooks who were threatening to put men and women out of work and cause mothers and babies to starve.

The reporters took notes. The photographers took pictures. This story was a natural.

As the press left, one reporter asked de Benedictis if he had fully calculated the possible consequences of his tough stand against helping the company.

"Perhaps a lighter paycheck for a short while is better than eventually having none at all?"

"You haven't understood what I said," replied the union leader, coldly turning away to resume his post on the wafer line.

He knew it wasn't the right moment to say more. As a Marxist, following the gradualist approach of the Italian road to socialism, you learned not to overplay it. He had scored against the Lazzaroni establishment. Good. But to say more, especially to that journalist, would risk losing what they had won.

Yet he could tell them more—plenty more. Work in a cookie factory was hell. When you stood on a production line, your hands and brain doing the same thing—over and over, all day long, month after month—it was destructive to the human mind and spirit. It eroded you on the inside and you had no way of halting it.

He would tell them:

"They complain of absenteeism—of workers staying at home for no good reason. And not only here. At the Fiat plant, they calculate one-third of the force is always missing. So costs go up, and Italy is going out of business.

"The Lazzaronis have a very dispiriting sign at the entrance, stating how many people don't show up each day, as though they were a bunch of traitors.

"It's true some workers fake it. Some take advantage of sick leave, and moonlight at other jobs. But only a few. The trouble here, and at Fiat and other factories, is the work atmosphere. It's the neurosis created inside the factory, by the rhythm of the work.

"A worker comes out stupid after eight hours of the same thing.

He feels tired, depressed. He needs rest. That's where absenteeism starts and it can only be stopped when they improve working conditions.

"That means not loading us up the way they do here. Twenty-six people have left for other jobs or family reasons. Pregnant women leave because they don't know what to do with the child, where to take it. We've calculated that another twenty will leave by next year ... but they haven't hired others to replace these. So the work force decreases, while production must remain the same. Human scales don't work like that. They have a limit and we have reached it here."

He would also tell them he was against violence, but it existed because it served the men who owned the factories.

"As a Communist, I don't believe in violence. It's not for us. It's an abuse of power and a suppression of respect for others. Violence is a dictatorship.

"The capitalist system wants it. They use violence to better control us—to keep workers and the young split apart. But it's a dangerous game. Unless they do something for labor and the youth, it will get worse and maybe go out of control.

"I can't understand why Berlinguer is collaborating with the Christian Democrats who have always been our enemy. For years they tell us one thing—and now another, with nothing getting better. The workers feel betrayed by their own party.

"Even so, I'd vote Communist again—but with a trembling hand."

LATE IN THE DAY, Delfino had another indication that the men holding Paolo Lazzaroni were among those in his registry of twenty-nine names suspected of forming the core of Kidnap Inc. Also, they were responsible for at least one other kidnapping. All this came from a report on the two men who had been picked up with a stolen car. Both of them—a Sicilian and a Calabrian—had family ties with others on Delfino's list.

This seemed to confirm his belief that the stolen car had been intended for use in a kidnapping. If so, the discovery had undoubtedly deferred the crime. It would probably continue to do so, until the gang knew whether or not the two men had squealed under interrogation.

He needed more data on the family relationships, and there was a chance of getting it from the two car thieves still in custody. He called the *questura,* where both men were being temporarily held, and requested permission to interrogate them. Times had changed. You couldn't simply question a crook. You had to wait until he got a lawyer. Of course, this protected innocent citizens against police abuse. But it was also a boon for criminals. They simply sat there and, through their lawyer, denied they had ever been born.

It delayed justice and was a waste of the taxpayers' money. In the old days, you caught a thief, took his confession, and sent him up for trial. You didn't have to always beat men to get them to talk. The police and carabinieri had strength and dignity of office. They represented the state and they were respected by criminals.

Delfino smiled, recalling his father and Il Tulu, a famous bandit suspected of many unproven crimes. Maresciallo Delfino summoned the suspect to the carabiniere command at Platì and read him a false telegram, naming Signor Tulu as an auxiliary carabiniere. Such an honor called for a banquet, and Maresciallo Delfino arranged one with plenty of wine. He also made ready a carabiniere uniform and had the bandit put it on. Looking at himself in the mirror, Tulu felt safe within the uniform—and within the law. He became transformed, as in a Pirandello play, and began to recount all his crimes, as well as those of others. When he had finished, Maresciallo Delfino slapped on the handcuffs, sent him to trial—and so to prison.

That was how it had been, and a bandit had talked. Today, with a lawyer, Tulu would never talk, and another crook would be free to turn children into drug addicts, terrorize his parents, and kill the police.

Yet even with a lawyer present, Delfino felt he could get the two car thieves to talk about their families—if only to protect the innocent members....

At that moment, the *questura* returned his call. They had checked on the two car thieves. Since the car owner had refused to press charges—especially after the defense lawyers had gotten to him—the magistrate had been unable to hold them. Both men had been released yesterday.

"Tell me," said Delfino, his voice flat with controlled anger. "Why didn't you let us know before you set them loose?"

"Ask the magistrate—not us. We do as told."

So did the Mafia. Obviously, a great deal depended on who was giving the order.

THURSDAY
The 11th Day

YOUR BROTHER GIGI is too smart for his own good!"

It was Bogey, angrily storming into the room before his usual hour.

"My brother?"

"Your brother. The damn fool got every stupid reporter in the country to scribble a lot of junk, with those jerky workers yapping away about losing their jobs because some big, bad crooks had taken their dear little Paolo away. They say they'll march on the prefect because we're going to make mothers and babies starve. What kind of Communist crap is that? You think we're against mothers and babies?"

Paolo tried to calm him down. He was feeling low—the effect of his confinement. Despite the exercises, his body was getting weaker. His eyes bothered him; the glaucoma was acting up. The stench was suffocating. His body itched.

Bogey began to pace back and forth. Pippo asked if he wanted a coffee, but he continued to rant against Gigi and the Lazzaroni employees.

"Them and their stinking commie unions! They're gonna teach us a lesson because you're gonna close down your plant to pay a ransom. What kind of horseshit is that? You've got money socked away in Switzerland—or somewhere. We know you've got it."

"We don't," said Paolo, quickly. "I keep trying to tell you that. We'd have to strain every asset we had to raise half a billion lire."

Bogey was quiet. Then, "No more?" he asked, suppressed tenseness in his voice.

"Maybe 750 million lire at the outside, but I doubt we could get it."

There, he had said it—a figure he hoped was near to what Anna and Gigi were quoting.

Bogey gave no further indication of whether this was acceptable or not. Instead, he continued his tirade against the workers.

"They're gonna march through the streets because we want to starve mothers and babies. The sons of bitches. If they march anywhere, we'll meet them with machine guns ... them and their commie lies."

"They won't march," said Paolo, trying to calm him down.

"You don't know how to handle workers. When you go back to your factory I'll give you a machine gun. That's the only thing that'll straighten them out, the pricks."

OUTSIDE: Bogey's anger was reflected in the first call toward midday. Luca Manzoni answered the phone at his father's home. The Caller said they didn't want any more Communists calling them names in the newspapers, and hung up. So that was a cover call, for the police.

The call to Renzo came later, at 10:30 P.M. After the password and a reply to the last question from Anna, Renzo jumped in at once to clarify their first ransom bid.

"Listen, the last time you hung up without letting me finish. I wanted to say that the sum I quoted was what the family had put aside on the first day, in liquid cash. Now that they're sure you have Paolo, they're doing what they can to raise more."

"You'd better get it, and get it fast," the Caller said.

"I must be truthful with you. Your initial request ... three billion lire ... it's absurd. We'll never be able to meet it."

For a moment he thought he had overplayed his hand. Was the

man going to hang up again? Then, through that familiar rustling of an imagined beard:

"Okay, our request is absurd. But your offer is also absurd. Do you realize what risks we're taking?... Make a bigger offer, and we'll see what we can do."

Then another unexpected remark:

"Tell Gigi to stop making a big stink in the papers. We don't like it and it's not good for Paolo's health. Understand?"

Renzo said he understood.

"Get your price up and we'll call tomorrow," said the Caller, hanging up.

Renzo had detected a note of urgency in the man's voice. Everyone agreed the bandits seemed to be in a greater hurry to settle—probably because of Gigi's press conference.

Anna was torn between tears and laughter. "Risks! Did you hear that? If they don't like taking risks, why go around kidnapping people?"

Returning home, she tried to decide on how much they should offer the kidnappers. Another small bid would drag it on for days, maybe weeks. Paolo would never be able to withstand that. It had to be terminated quickly with a sizable bid. The captors were ready for it—but how much?

She was undressing when the phone rang—startling her.

"Mommie?"

It was Luca calling from the chalet—at this hour, after midnight. Oh, dear God, they were hurt!

"Mommie, you didn't call us for the goodnight kiss."

"I'm sorry. But it's rather late now for you to be up.

"Are you both in bed?"

"No, we're by the phone and Franca's asleep. Marco wants a kiss, too."

There followed the sound of both children kissing the phone. Then Marco spoke.

"Is Daddy home, Mommie?"

"No, he's still on his trip. But he'll be here soon."

"For Easter, maybe?"

"Yes, I hope so."

"You see? I told you!" cried Marco.

Luca took the phone. "Is it true, Mommie? We'll have the big Easter hunt like always?"

"Yes, I hope so. Say your prayers for it tonight. Now go on to bed, both of you."

"Goodnight, Mommina!"

In bed, she turned off the light.

"Goodnight, little loves," she said. Then holding herself, she spoke to Paolo: "Goodnight, darling, I love you ... love you."

DELFINO WAS AT HOME with Carla and his children when the recording center called him and replayed the talk between Renzo and the Caller.

It was perfect. He now had what he wanted. By tapping every line in the apartment house, he had found the "safe phone." What's more, it seemed the bandits were anxious to discuss terms. In fact, they seemed in a greater hurry than usual.

Why? Did they believe that Gigi's press conference would put greater heat on them? No, it wasn't that. They were angry. Their superegos—containing both the strength and weakness of the criminal personality—had been insulted. Yet it wasn't that or fear which was driving them to close the deal. It was something else—but what?

Maybe a forced confession of Antonio had alarmed them. If they knew that Major Delfino had compiled a list of names from informants and was preparing to arrest them all in one night, they would clear out of town—without even knowing who was actually on the list. Before leaving, they would get as much ransom as possible from the hostages in hand. They would then flee.to other cities or remote towns until the danger passed—until Delfino was killed, or until he had arrested whoever was dumb enough to stay behind.

This could explain their haste. If so, Paolo Lazzaroni and any other hostage still alive were in extreme danger. Failing to get the ransom (or even with it), the fleeing kidnappers would be forced to release their charges—or kill them.

A wholesale release would bring joy to many homes and a

lowering of tension in countless others. This was exactly what the kidnappers did not want. Their long-range goal—not generally known—was not merely to kidnap one or two rich men each month. It was, instead, to raise the level of terror to the point where large sums would be paid without having to undergo the risk and expense of a proper kidnapping. The basic cost had risen. The entire operation—surveillance of victim, importing and exporting pickup men, care and custody, callers and runners for contacts—now cost about $340,000 in lire. Besides this, the private banks took 40 percent in recycling ransom money, which was registered on computer drums with the Bank of Italy.

All of this could be avoided, with less risk to both kidnappers and hostages, if the potential victim would be sensible and pay protection money. It could vary between 5 and 10 million a year—even more for someone as rich as the Agnellis who owned the Fiat Motor Company.

So they were paying. Scores and perhaps hundreds of families—the exact number was not known—had come to terms with kidnappers. They paid to live in peace, without need to send their children to school abroad nor abandon their business firms to live in New York or Brazil. The annual take in Italian kidnappings ran close to $18 million a year; the "silent" payment of protection money was estimated at double the amount—with still more to come. By raising the level of terror, the Mafia and the 'ndrangheta expected to triple the current sum to a yearly outlay of $55 million in lire. Besides the effect of such sums going into drugs and prostitution—creating cancer pockets within the social body—this was a severe drain on private industry, restricting or halting renewal and development. In this way, the nation became progressively weaker as the cancer spread.

The government in Rome would continue to do nothing about it until its members were personally threatened. The Mafia, however, would never allow that to happen—to awaken those who slept in special privilege, or those who had been elected by Mafia interests. The only real threats to the government would come from left- or right-wing terrorist groups. The Mafia, like runaway cancer cells, existed and multiplied within a living body. As long as the body remained alive, so did the tumor. The goal of the terrorists—especially the Red Brigades—was to destroy the state and its institutions in order to restructure them in a dictatorship of the proletariat.

The Red Brigades were already maiming and killing editors, judges, members of the police force. Sooner or later, they would begin to strike at major political figures—ministers or cabinet members—as had happened elsewhere in Argentina, Germany, Japan. When that happened in Italy, the Mafia could be expected to try and save its own existence by saving the host body—those existing institutions and government bodies which had allowed it to flourish.

They would turn against the Red Brigades, or any allied terrorist group, and secretly begin to destroy them. They would murder those in prisons and they would infiltrate those on the outside to destroy their unity—or reveal them to the police. They would accomplish this with their usual skill, discipline, and silence—moving with such secrecy that historians would not know about it until years later, if ever.

FRIDAY
The 12th Day

N HIS SLEEP, he remembered the name of the medicine, and woke up.

"Pippo?"

"Yes, Paolo."

"Listen, write this down before I forget it. Bellergal." He spelled it out. "You got it? If my heart goes into this ... irregularity, I'll need it immediately."

"Sure, Paolo, we'll get it for you. Don't worry."

OUTSIDE: Anna, Gigi, and Manzoni now realized they were at a crucial point. The bandits had asked for a higher bid, something high enough to be accepted quickly.

How much should it be? The general rule was for a moderate raise—certainly not to jump from 150 million lire to, say, 500 million. If they did that, the bandits might feel they could get still more. On the other hand, if they made it too small, the negotiations would drag out, and Paolo's life would be endangered.

Also, why were the bandits in a hurry? Maybe they felt Delfino closing in on them. If so, they might move Paolo, risking his life. Or Delfino might try to raid their hideout—again a risk to Paolo. Or perhaps they were quarreling among themselves. In Rome, one band had broken apart and shot each other in front of a woman hostage who then, miraculously, staggered out onto the street—free without any ransom.

That evening they were ready with a prepared text for Renzo, offering 600 million lire. Anna was unusually nervous. She had helped prepare the note. Yet now, as they waited for the call from the bandits, she sensed it was wrong. They were not offering enough.

The phone rang and she acted on instinct. Grabbing the note, she raised the figure to 730 million. Her spontaneous addition made the offer almost identical with the amount Paolo told Bogey would be the family limit.

The figure was now close to one million dollars. Renzo told the Caller it was the absolute maximum. He wanted to close the deal before the workers marched on the prefect of police. Also, the papers were saying the attorney general was about to block the Lazzaroni funds.

"So we have to act now, or there won't be anything."

"Make it a round seven-fifty," said the Caller. "What's a few more million to you?"

Renzo knew he had them.

"This is our limit, friend. You have to believe us."

"We'll consider it and let you know tomorrow."

HEARING THE PLAYBACK, Delfino knew they would take it. The offer was good. It allowed for an end to bargaining and immediate payment. Yet what was driving the bandits to close so fast? Was it, as he had suspected, fear of future arrest? A result of Antonio telling them of Delfino's list of names? Somehow this was too gross, too easy to be credible.

Paolo was still alive; so it wasn't that which caused them to hasten. Nor did they want the money to kill him. These were Calabrians. Usually they didn't kill hostages, unless their faces were seen or unless they were tricked. Besides, it wasn't good business. . . .

Good business? Of course, that was it. A lower ransom price

would speed up the payment and also explain the recent increase in kidnappings. It was like any chain-store operation. A rapid turnover at a lower profit could bring more money than a slower turnover with greater overhead. Holding out for, say, three billion lire meant that talks might drag on for two or three months. They could do three kidnappings in the same period. Also, the longer the holding time, the greater the risk of being discovered by the police or of losing the hostage through an accident or lack of proper medical care. It was a new technique that made sense: Less risk and more profit.

SATURDAY
The 13th Day

HIS STRENGTH was leaving him. He had tried to conserve it, but it was slipping away. Each day he had felt it happening, and this morning, in rising off the chamber pot, he had nearly collapsed. Back in bed, he had started his isometric exercises, but his arms and legs were too heavy and he had given it up.

He had to gain control of himself, and in his mind he began to write another letter to his son, Luca. Then he wrote one for Marco—letters telling them how much he loved them and how, by fixing on this love, he was able to endure the darkness and maintain hope that one day he would see them again.

After that, he began to think about a machine they needed at the factory. One of their most famous products was a tin of assorted cookies. Packaging them required forty-two women on an assembly line. They needed a machine to take over this work, but until now no one had been able to invent one. Cookies are both friable and variable in size. So metal claws or prongs could not be used on them.

It would have to be a drop system. The cookies could move along a belt, then drop through the proper holes. They could kidnap themselves. *Kidnapped cookies,* he thought ... and at that moment his heart went out of rhythm.

For a moment it seemed to stop altogether—as though an electric plug had been pulled out and the heart itself had collapsed: *aaahhh!*—followed by the organ struggling to live on, grasping for life with irregular double beats: *Two-two, two-two, two-two* ...

"Pippo! ... Pippo!"

Basso came shuffling into the room. You could tell it was he. Pippo walked lightly.

"Where's Pippo?"

"Buying some groceries."

"Where's the medicine for my heart? I need it fast."

"What medicine?"

"I told Pippo. He wrote it down. It's called ... Bella ... no, Bellergal. It must be there. Go look."

After a bit, Basso came back.

"Can't find anything. Would it be a bottle?"

Paolo nodded.

"Nothing. But don't worry, Pippo will be back soon."

"I need it now, fast.... Please, can't you go get me some?"

"I'm sorry, Paolo, I can't leave you alone. I'm the guard."

"Listen ... it's urgent ... my heart."

"Paolo, if they find me gone, they might kill me. You understand?"

Oh, God.... *Two-two, two-two, two-two.* ...

"Can't you hold out a little bit?"

He had to. He tried to breathe deeply and lie still. Maybe it would pass. If he lay perfectly quiet, maybe it would go away.

His mind strayed again, and he had to smile. In a way, he wasn't alone. He was like all of Italy: In the dark, organism weakening, heart going crazy, yet holding out.

Two-two, two-two ...

He closed his eyes and for a moment felt Anna next to him. He could feel her body, her heart beating with his, her mouth opening, both of them breathing together now ... yes, like that, yes, my love, yes....

OUTSIDE: When the bandits called, there was no further bargaining. The papers had reported the Lazzaroni wealth was now blocked by order of the attorney general.

"We can't get any more now," said Renzo.

The Caller went into detail about the size of the bills. Lire notes of 100,000 would be all right, but not in serial.

"No funny stuff," he said. "No marked money. Remember, we're going to look it over before we let Paolo go."

He also explained how the bills were to be divided into different packs. The entire lot was to be delivered in a blue Italian Navy seabag.

Anna then prompted Renzo to make two final requests.

"Look," said Renzo. "We've given you the utmost collaboration ... and now we're friends. So why can't we wind this up American-style—cash on delivery? Swap person for money—all at once?"

"Impossible," replied the Caller. "We need two days to check out the money."

Renzo then asked for another photo, which was also refused.

"We answered your last question. You know Paolo's alive. Actually, he had a bit of heart trouble, but it's okay now. We got him the medicine he asked for and his ticker's doing fine ... like a champ."

Anna, listening on a separate phone, felt her own heart skip a beat. Paolo had his trouble again! She had known it was going to happen. It meant he was losing his strength. Once this began, nothing would save him—unless he came home. They had to end this quickly ... now.

The Caller was imparting final instructions.

"Get the stuff and tell us tomorrow when you can deliver. The sooner the better for you. Remember what I said. Screw this up and you'll never see Paolo again."

DELFINO, monitoring the taped talk, knew the next call would set the date of delivery—but not reveal how or where it was to be delivered.

That was too important to risk over the phone. It would come another way, perhaps by hand-carried letter. Gigi might find it in his mailbox, on his desk at the office, on the front seat of his car. Or it would go to Manzoni. Or to the sister, Pia. Or even Anna. It didn't matter. There were a hundred ways to get a message through to the family without anyone knowing it. You would need a hundred men to cover all of them—and even then it wouldn't be certain. Besides, it was important to let the instructions come through, so they could then enter the final phase. There was time enough to learn how it was going to be delivered. And there were also ways to do it.

He replayed the tape and shook his head with admiration. That Anna was running the whole show. She was one helluva woman. Carla was like that. You could count on her for anything.

One night, driving through Luino, he had seen a man carrying shoe boxes from a store to a truck. It was after midnight, and obviously this was a robbery. He raced to the jailhouse of the small town and found only one carabiniere on duty. Since no one else would remain to guard the jail, he swore in Carla as an auxiliary. Then he handed her a .38 Special and called her by her maiden name.

"Auxiliary Valsesia! Take your post!"

"Si, Signor Tenente!"

So he had left her, with pistol in hand, holding the jailhouse, while he and the local carabiniere made the arrest.

Italy was held together by its women. In many ways, they could take more than their men, yet never break. Under duress, they were probably the most formidable women in the world.

SUNDAY
The 14th Day

THE MEDICINE had corrected his heart rhythm, but it left him weak and depressed. He didn't want to think about it, fearing it would cause another attack, and he tried to make another "escape"—retracing one of his many trips to Africa or India. His mind wandered, however, and he found his thoughts returning to Anna and the children.

Easter was only one week away. They had always had such fun together on Easter—the whole family, with his parents and Gigi and Pucci, the boys and girls and the many cousins. He could see them now so clearly—the children searching for the hidden eggs, turning about like startled forest deer, the sun in their hair, the wind blowing little skirts, their shadows shifting round and about as they ran across the lawn, then down to the woods and into the dark shadows with sudden squeals of joy and laughter.

He slipped back further in time, finding himself a small boy at the old convent home of his parents at Saronno—waiting for the arrival of San Nicolao with his Christmas gifts. In order to see him first, he had snuck out of the main house and into the conservatory room. It was nearest to the garden and, from the window where he stood, he would see San Nicolao as soon as he came upon the gravel path.

It was going to be hard for him to find everybody. The sky was covered with clouds and dark wisps of fog twirled about in the light coming from the living room where all the others sat waiting for him. Silly fools, sitting there like melons. He alone knew how to spy from this advanced post, this dark, unheated room jutting out into the garden.

The window was almost too high, but by standing on his toes, he could see through the bottom of the lower pane. His breath fogged it over, and when he wiped it, water ran down the glass and remained on his hand. There was a smell to it and to the cold air coming through the window, mixed with the odor of wood smoke from the laundry. It was the sharp, clean smell of winter and of snow about to fall. He breathed in and felt it going deep into his lungs, then up his back and into his head—remaining there, low and still, like a sleeping fog.

When the fog came, everyone was happy. They smiled and they held each other, and it was more fun in the house. When the sky was clear and full of blue-white stars, the bomber planes would come to drop their bombs on families and children and make the city cry out, its sirens screaming, the searchlights reaching up into the sky like fingers of a wounded giant, blind and helpless, grasping to the stars for help, while everyone ran in pajamas and slippers into the shelter—everyone, that is, except Captain Scotty. The Englishman, thin as a girl, had appeared on the back lawn one clear night, hiding his parachute in the tool shed until it reappeared later as nightgowns and blouses for the Swiss nanny, who happily accepted silk for nothing, while his mother wore it with pride—especially after Scotty set up a machine gun to fire upon a German convoy.

Why had it taken him so long to learn about his mother, to read her eyes? They belonged to San Nicolao, but he didn't see it, wasn't looking, never did.

At the window, his body chilled, his legs cramped, he began to fear that San Nicolao would never find them. He had never been here before. It had always happened in Milan, in the chapel of the nuns on Via Boscovich, everyone waiting for him in one place—by the blue glass windows with white stars—until he came with two angels, one carrying a broom, the other something else. But now the war had scattered them everywhere. Uberto and Cicci were at Varese, Sandro Minghetti in Switzerland. At least San Nicolao could use a sled there, looking for all the dispersed children in the snow and fog and rain.

Outside, on the road to the factory, there was the rumble of old Masini slowing his big truck down for the turn. It happened all day, but at night it was scary because the rumble sounded like the bomber planes. The truck faded away and he heard it then—the first sounds of the bell, tinkling, as though coming across distant fields, or maybe from heaven. He listened: Again the tinkling. *Dio!* He was getting nearer!

Running through the dark conservatory, he burst into the bright light of the living room, seeing them all in an instant: Gigi, Pia, Pina Valsecchi, Anna Lombardi, Marisa, little Augusta, the governess, Sister Anny, and, near the door, Enrica and Alda holding some tiny sandals to give to San Nicolao for his angels.

"He's coming! I heard him in the garden!"

Now they were all standing, huddled together and whispering, hands reaching for each other, eyes bright with excitement, staring at the door as the bell came closer.

Din-din ... din-din ... din-DIN!... DIN-DIN!

O Dio, now ... now.... Then the door opening slowly as he entered, wearing the brown Franciscan robe, the cowl low over his face to protect him from the cold. Slowly the face lifted up—and then the eyes! His hand was there, too, touching, holding yours, speaking with a voice like silver, telling them how sad it was along the road where he had seen much hunger and destruction and sorrow—and so many little boys and girls lost without mothers and fathers or anywhere to sleep.

Then he told them a story about how it was once, in another world that had been happy, like this one—until it, too, fell into war. Bombs fell on cities, children were left alone, wandering the streets without homes. Men hated each other, and there was everywhere a lament and a weeping for what had been lost.

San Nicolao smiled and nodded to the children now sitting around him on the living-room floor, no one blinking for fear of missing a fraction of a moment. Then he told them what had happened.

The first child appeared without anyone expecting him. They saw the sun golden on his hair, the smiling face, the blinking eyes, the little feet without shoes ... and then, held high, the bright flower. Behind the first one came another one, then another, and another—until there was a river of children, each one holding a flower, flowing across the land and into the valleys.

Everywhere they went, the men and women who saw them would come out of their places of hiding, clasping hands and looking into each others' eyes and hearts. The men then returned to their fields, to make them fertile again. The women ceased to weep and began to laugh and put their homes in order.

So it went. Everywhere across the land, wherever the children came with their flowers held high, their faces turned upward with smiles and laughter—everywhere they passed, there was joy and rejoicing....

"Paolo?"

"Yes, Pippo?"

"You feeling better?"

"Yes, I think so."

"Your heart, it's okay now?"

"It's finding its way ... the old way."

"Good, Paolo. I was worried."

"Thank you, dear friend."

He would see them first. Before all other men. Pippo would see the first child to come forth holding a flower.

OUTSIDE: Major Delfino had phoned, saying it was urgent, and Anna was dressing to meet him. She took out a bright spring outfit—powder-blue suede skirt and beige blouse with puff sleeves. Putting on a pearl necklace with earrings, she realized she was making herself pretty for the first time in many days. But for whom? A carabiniere major! Well—why not? It never hurt to look pretty. And God only knew what he wanted.

Before leaving, she looked at herself again in the mirror. She had to have her hair done soon. Maybe Paolo would be home in the next few days. She had to start taking care of herself again. Her nails, too.... And some flowers around the house.

At the carabiniere headquarters, Delfino also seemed to know that Paolo was about to be released.

"I'm aware, Signora, that you're about to withdraw a large sum of money to pay Paolo's ransom. It's a lot of money, maybe too much."

"I know nothing about it," she replied. "You have to talk with Avvocato Manzoni or my brother-in-law."

"If that's true, they're keeping secrets from you, and we must do something about it immediately." He paused. "It's very dangerous to keep a lady in the dark."

She smiled at that, and for a moment they relaxed. He was, she knew, a good man—even an admirable one and very brave. He was trying to do the best he could for them. But she had to be careful. He wanted something, and she knew it was going to be difficult.

"I don't want you to pay the ransom now. In a few more days, we will probably be able to free Paolo without paying anything. We have information and will soon know where he is being kept."

"No, Signor Maggiore. We can't wait. It's impossible."

"Why?"

"We want Paolo home for Easter. I promised the children."

"You can tell them he's been delayed. He'll come a week later. Also, it's more secure this way. You have no assurance they will return Paolo, even after you pay the ransom. But if we locate the hideout, we'll get them all—Paolo and the bandits—and you'll pay nothing."

Nothing, she thought, except maybe Paolo's life if they had a shoot-out.

"No, I'm sorry. I know you're trying to help us. We want to cooperate. But in this, we cannot. I want Paolo home for Easter."

"Why don't you trust me?"

"I have to trust myself in this. Something tells me that if he's not home for Easter ... he'll never come home again."

She was close to tears and knew she had to leave.

"Please, may I go?"

"Yes, Signora. Tell your brother-in-law and Avvocato Manzoni that I expect to be informed of all details before they go out to pay the ransom. That's our agreement, and I expect them to keep it."

RENZO received a call with grim warnings.

"Where's the stuff?"

"We'll have it ready by tomorrow at 6 P.M. Okay?"

"Remember this, mister. No marked money. Do exactly as we tell you, or it's goodbye Paolo."

"What do we do?"

"Get a Fiat 600, or a 126. Nothing bigger. Put a baggage rack on it."

"Then what?"

"Just get it and have it ready with the stuff. We'll tell you the rest tomorrow. Let me warn you for the last time ... if we see one lousy cop, we bury Paolo in cement."

DELFINO flicked off the recording. So it was exactly as he had anticipated. The final details would not be communicated by phone. Those pros wouldn't take the risk—even an outside risk, no matter how small—that, in spite of everything, the cops had found the safe line. They'd use some other channel.

He had to know. The gang chiefs picked up the ransom money themselves, trusting no one. He had to be there. Not to capture them—that could mean a dead Paolo—but to photograph them from a distance with night cameras. He had already covered three ransom payments that way, with camera lens and with gunsight. He could have killed every bandit at that moment. If the rate of kidnapping increased—especially with the Red Brigades who this week in Rome were asking 1.5 billion lire for release of shipbuilder Piero Costa—the public might angrily demand that these men be killed, if not on the spot, then after capture and a trial.

There were ways to reach the place of ransom payment, other than being told by the family, but it was more secure with their cooperation. Avvocato Manzoni would be the best man. A lawyer was always more conscious of his legal obligations. He would tell him he knew the ransom was to be delivered the next day, and the law required that the carabinieri be kept informed of all details, as soon as they were known.

He phoned Manzoni, but there was no answer. He tried several times later—still no reply. Had Manzoni's legal mind anticipated this? Was he lying low, knowing the major was about to bind him by law?

He tried calling Anna but the maid, Diomira, said the signora was out, and she didn't know when she was coming home. So all three of them were out. That meant they were together, probably in Manzoni's office preparing for tomorrow. He would get them then. There was still time.

MONDAY
The 15th Day

IT WAS A DAY no one would forget—no one, on either side of the law.

First, the ransom money had to be withdrawn from the bank, where it had been placed in a manner to allow for its legal withdrawal. It would be quite a bundle—730 million lire in cash. They had to walk in, pick it up—and walk out in broad daylight. How could this be done with minimal risk of its being hijacked by a rival gang? Or caught by Delfino's carabinieri, who could confiscate funds destined for criminals? Either way, a delay in delivery might cause the bandits to kill Paolo.

Shortly after 10 A.M., a car pulled up before a bank near the La Scala opera house. Anna's brother Marco sauntered into the bank. Then another car pulled up, and another young man got out and went into the bank. Finally, an attractive young woman with a Vuitton shopping bag strolled down the sidewalk. She stopped in front of the bank, searched through her pocketbook, and, as though on an impulse, went inside.

A few minutes later, Marco came out with a bundle that looked for all the world like a bundle of banknotes. Furtively, he crossed the sidewalk, got into his car and sped away. A few minutes later, the second youth emerged, carrying another package. Looking up and down the street with an air of one who knew what he was about, he, too, got into his car and drove off. Five minutes later, the young woman came out, and proceeded casually on her way. She paused before a shop window, then stepped absent-mindedly into a waiting chauffeured limousine. There was no tenseness, such as might be natural to someone with close to a million dollars in lire in her shopping bag. The vehicle eased into the traffic.

That evening, Anna, Gigi, and Renzo sat by the phone in Renzo's apartment. They had a blue Italian Navy seabag with 730 million lire inside. They also had an identical bag, stuffed with four Milan phone books, in the event of a hijacking. A rented Fiat 126, with baggage rack, was parked outside, near the apartment house.

All they lacked now were instructions on how to deliver the ransom. Finally the phone rang at 6:04 P.M. The Caller spoke quickly, as though suspecting Major Delfino had finally managed to tap this phone.

"Go immediately to Piazza Fratellini Zavatari. At number six, there's an auto school—Santangelo. In front of it, there's a phone booth with four phone books. In the fourth one you'll find a message telling you what to do. Is that clear?"

"Yes," replied Renzo.

"Move fast. Hurry. We'll call you when you get back."

"How will you know when that is?"

"Don't ask stupid questions. Get moving."

Gigi leaped into his Rover and raced to the piazza. It was raining and dark, and the piazza seemed desolate at night. The juncture of several highways, it had the wasted aspect of a field after a circus has pulled up its tents and gone away.

Then he saw the yellow sign: Autoscuola Santangelo. And there was a phone booth.

Leaving his car double-parked, motor running, Gigi ran for the booth—only to discover it occupied by two men. *Madonna!* Delfino had tapped the phone and his men were already there!

Gigi waited nervously, pretending to look at the auto school window. The two men came out and walked away. Gigi decided they were carabinieri in civvies. You could tell a cop anywhere.

He sidled into the booth and found his fears confirmed. There were only three telephone books. The fourth book from the right had been ripped out. Jesus! They had been out-maneuvered by Major Delfino! Desperately, he flipped through the third book, hoping there had been a miscount. Nothing!

The bandits would be calling again, and he sped back to the house to report the disaster. For a moment, no one spoke. Then Anna said, "The fourth book was missing?"

"Yes."

"From the left or from the right?"

Without a word, they both ran for Gigi's car. Back at the phone booth, counting from left to right this time, and allowing for the missing book, they found a folded note taped to the inside of the back cover.

Gigi tore it open. This was it!

In the half-light, they could just make out the hand-printed instructions: Place a demijohn in the baggage rack. (But the word "demijohn" had been crossed out and the word "mattress" written in.) Go to the Piazza Kennedy and follow the route on the hand-scrawled map, traveling always at 60 kilometers an hour. (The figure 60 was changed to 70.)

"Come on, this is it!" cried Gigi.

"Let me see it again," said Anna, inside the car.

The instructions were to drive out toward Saronno then back toward Milan along the highway to Rome, then back again to Milan—a circuit of 200 kilometers. Presumably, they would stop somewhere along this route to hand over the money. But where?

Back at the apartment, the phone rang again. It was the Caller.

"You got the instructions?"

"Yes," replied Renzo. "But how will we know where to stop?"

"Just keep driving. We'll let you know when to stop."

It was no job for Anna, or for Gigi, for that matter. So Renzo had provided a driver named Franco. Another trusted man, Renato, well known to the Lazzaronis, would accompany him.

It was raining when the two men began the trip, both in the front seat of the small car. On the floor between their legs were two heavy bags: One with the money, the other with four Milan phone books. Above them, tied to the baggage rack, was a blue flower-print mattress taken from Renzo's guest room. It was partially covered by transparent nylon.

The little red car, with the rolled-up mattress, made its way slowly through Milan traffic toward the Saronno highway. The rain came down in torrents and very soon the mattress was soaked. Other motorists looked at it and shook their heads. How stupid could anyone be to take a brand-new mattress out into a rainstorm?

Coming off the highway exit at Saronno, they ran into a carabiniere roadblock.

"God help us," said Franco.

"Madonna," said Renato, in a secondary form of prayer.

Bending over in the rain, a carabiniere peered into the car window.

"Where you going?"

"Just up the road," replied Franco. "My friend lives there. We're in a hurry ... the mattress is getting wet."

"It sure as hell is," said the cop. "Why didn't you cover it up ... where are your papers?"

There were no papers. Franco had neglected to bring his driver's license. Now they were in for it. They'd have to get out, and the cops would see the bags.

"Let him go," said another cop. "That mattress is getting ruined."

They waved them on.

AVVOCATO MANZONI came home from an early dinner to find his phone ringing—on and on. He ran to it, certain that this was something important. Maybe the bandits were going to threaten him with Paolo's death. Fumbling with the tape recorder connected to the phone, he pressed the wrong button, and Delfino's voice bellowed from the speakers.

"MANZONI! MANZONI!"

"Yes, Major?"

"YOU HAVE BETRAYED ME!"

Manzoni looked up at the ceiling. The major's voice was bouncing off it like the judgment of God.

"I'm sorry, Major. What have I done?"

Delfino said he understood the ransom money was being delivered that night—where was the route information? Manzoni said he knew nothing about it but would try to find out.

Manzoni really didn't know. By mutual consent, he had been detached from the triumvirate. It had been agreed among them that, as a lawyer, he would be hard put to lie if Delfino called him in for information. And they sensed that that could happen at any time. They had seen too many signs of police watchfulness outside their houses to imagine that the major had been sitting on his hands. So they had agreed that Manzoni would stop coming to their nightly meetings and would not be told of what was going on.

Now he had to find out—or at least go through the motions. First, he could look for Gigi. Gigi usually dined at his golf club outside of town. Manzoni drove there.

Gigi wasn't at the club. Manzoni drove back. He had consumed a whole hour. Good. Now to look for Anna. That—if she was making the right moves—should take up more time. *Bene....*

FRANCO AND RENATO were in another mess. The instructions said to curve back onto the highway at the same Saronno junction. Yet how could they go through the roadblock again?

Fortunately, Renato knew the area and guided Franco through back roads until they reached the next exit at Turati. Here, they entered the highway and began to drive at the prescribed speed of 70 kilometers per hour.

After a short distance, they found themselves boxed in between two cars. The one in front had a rear fog light turned on, without need for it in the rain. Each time Franco slowed down, the car ahead slowed down. The one behind remained on their tail.

"That's them," said Franco.

"We're back in business," agreed Renato.

So they went for several kilometers, until suddenly the car in front raced off, followed by the one in the rear. They had the highway all to themselves—two men in a tiny red Fiat with a blue mattress rolled up on top, and one million dollars in lire between their legs. Then another car pulled up alongside, forced them over to the side of the road and stopped just ahead. Franco stopped, too.

A hooded figure leaped out and ran up to them.

"Justus," the man said.

He wore a black woolen hood and his eyes were dark.

"I said Justus! Where is it?"

Renato and Franco knew this was it. They gave him the bag with the money.

"Don't move from here for ten minutes," the man said, running back to his car.

GIGI HAD TAKEN CARE to make it difficult for the police or Manzoni or anyone else to find him by going to a friend's house for dinner. Manzoni finally located Anna, and was able, by 9 P.M., to proceed unhurriedly to the carabiniere headquarters to tell Delfino of the ransom arrangements. By that time, however, it didn't matter: Gigi had received a call from Renzo: "Mission accomplished."

IT DIDN'T MATTER, either, to Major Delfino whose men had followed the entire operation without anyone knowing it.

To achieve this, everything possible was done to conceal the true identity of the carabinieri in their squad cars. They wore civilian clothes, appearing variously as successful businessmen, work-weary laborers, middle-class university students, or bushy-haired hippies. They drove a variety of cars, commensurate with their stations in life, without any indication that their cars were bulletproof in critical areas and contained high-powered, two-way radios, special defense and attack weapons, night cameras, and an assortment of other gadgets to help them along the way.

There was no difficulty in following the ransom car when it left to meet the bandits. By telescoping onto Renzo's apartment house, they observed everyone entering and leaving. From the phone tap, they knew to expect a Fiat 600 or 126 with an empty baggage rack. It arrived, a cozy little red 126, the night before, and was parked near the entrance.

When Franco and Renato came out into the rain with the blue mattress—covering it partially with transparent nylon—they knew this was a signal to identify the car for the bandits. And when the two men emerged again bearing two blue seabags—Anna watching nervously through the glass door of the building—they knew this was the ransom money and the operation was about to begin.

After the tiny Fiat pulled out, it was followed by the carabinieri in their various cars. One car would tail it for a while, then pass to allow another one to take its place. There were a dozen of them, linked by radio with each other and with Major Delfino who had remained at headquarters to better direct the operation—and, in a spare moment, to raise hell with Avvocato Manzoni for failing to keep him informed.

When the little Fiat reached the superhighway, traveling at a slow 70 kilometers per hour with the blue mattress on top and its nylon flapping in the rain, it was as easy to follow as a fish in an aquarium tank. At the Saronno roadblock, however, there was some difficulty and fast scrambling. Unaware that the Fiat was due to return to the highway, the carabinieri now faced the task of following the little car on backcountry roads, where concealment was infinitely more difficult.

Four cars were quickly called into action. Two followed the little Fiat—the first one soon passing on ahead, and keeping a far lead, while the second one lay as far back as possible. The third car exited at Turati, heading back toward the Saronno exit. The fourth waited at Turati. When car No. 3 approached No. 2, heading for Turati with the Fiat behind it, Delfino's men knew they were again in control. Finally, Car No. 4 picked up the Fiat as it came onto the highway.

So it went until Franco and Renato were boxed in by two bandit cars. When these two suddenly zoomed off—with no indication of whether or not they were alerted to the presence of police—the carabinieri cars nearest to the Fiat gave chase. Car No. 3, aware of its position, lay further back—holding control by going at the same speed as the ransom car—until it came upon the red Fiat and saw it had stopped behind a powerful Volvo at the edge of the highway.

Car No. 3 continued on down the highway, holding its fixed speed, until the Volvo raced by—obviously with the ransom money.

This was broadcast in code to all cars, including the first two which were still following the original escort vehicles which had run off.

In this manner, Delfino's men tracked the bandits to a small restaurant on the outskirts of Milan. Two agents left their cars and entered. It was a neighborhood trattoria, and the two men, obvious strangers, were watched with suspicion by the owner. Finally, from their conduct and speech, he determined that these were two homosexuals. They ordered some wine and he accepted it with a nod. Turning away, he glanced at a corner table—closing his eyes slowly to indicate it was all right.

Four men were seated at the table. Two of them were later identified from photographs as being on Delfino's list of suspects in Kidnap Inc. The other two eventually made the same list—raising it to thirty-four names.

TUESDAY
The 16th Day

T WAS the second day that Bogey had failed to pick up the necessary answer for Anna. It had happened once before, in the beginning, and at that time Pippo and Basso had shouted at each other. Now it was different. There were no fights and all was calm—too calm, somehow. It made him uneasy, and in bed he thought of a ship becalmed on a flat sea, abandoned, and lost.

If Bogey did not return it meant they were no longer talking with Anna. If so, they might have been paid off and were going to release him—or kill him. Or else, they had broken off the talks and were now going to let him rot in this room—or, again, kill him.

Some kidnap victims had been killed after the bandits had received the ransom. Or else, after being paid the agreed price, they asked for more. When that happened, the family sometimes assumed the victim was dead and refused to pay more. Or they were unable to raise the additional sum, and the bandits killed their hostage.

He felt a tightening around his heart and reached under the bed for the bottle of heart pills with a standing glass of water. He was already taking the maximum of six tablets a day. But if he took only one more now, he could skip one later.

Pippo probably knew what was going on and why Bogey hadn't come. Or did he? They never talked about the ransom or anything connected with it. When Pippo brought him dinner, however, he tried to get some indication of what was happening.

"Is there another question from my wife? I'm ready to answer it."

"Okay."

"Maybe they'll want it tomorrow?"

"Maybe. I don't know."

Pippo walked out, and Paolo realized it had been a mistake. Either Pippo didn't know, or he knew and was worried, too.

If they were going to kill him, Pippo would not want to do it. It would have to be Basso or someone else. And it probably would happen at night. They would come in suddenly and do it while he was asleep. Or they would make him stand up and take him away to where they were going to leave him—in some hole or in a lake without tides to wash up the body.

OUTSIDE: The bandits would phone, or Paolo would call from a public booth, after they had released him. Either way, he had to be picked up quickly, before Delfino grabbed him for questioning. Paolo could talk to him later, when he had recovered.

To insure this, Anna with Gigi and Aurelio had organized friends, relatives, and factory employees to remain near phones in separate areas of Milan and at Saronno where Paolo had been kidnapped. When the call came through, giving Paolo's location, it would be relayed by phone to whomever was nearest to him. Depending upon where this would be, they planned to reach Paolo in from three to fifteen minutes. Unless someone spotted Paolo and called a squad car, Delfino, didn't have a chance.

Waiting by their phones, Anna and Gigi and Aurelio found this to be the worst ordeal of all. For fifteen days they had driven on, without rest, doing everything possible to save Paolo. Yet now, with the ransom paid and their cars waiting, they found themselves totally unprepared for the agony of the wait. Each time the phone rang, they would leap for it, hearts pounding, the mind racing onward, saying this was it, this had to be the voice of the Caller they all knew so well and would hear forever in their dreams—only to find it was one of their own voices, unable to bear the isolation of waiting, the growing weight of the silent phone.

Why weren't the bandits calling? Why did they need two days to count the ransom money? Had they killed Paolo? Had they buried him somewhere? Would they call again and say they wanted more money? What if they never called—not tomorrow, nor the day after, nor ever again?

Unable to bear this—the fear of the future or the tension of the present—they found their thoughts turning elsewhere, toward themselves and their own lives.

Gigi looked at his phone and had the sensation of struggling to awaken from a nightmare. He was just below the surface, trying to open his eyes—only to be pulled back again into darkness and terror. It would not last. It had to end soon, when the phone rang and he heard his brother's voice: "Hello, Gigi?"

It would be over then—for them. But the nightmare would continue for other families on the kidnappers' list. It was a disease in the body of Italy, and it reflected a bigger disease in the body of Europe. There was a loss of direction and purpose, a paralysis of institutions to cope with the new forces of crisis. Growing masses of people, existing outside of society, wanted to destroy it with left-wing terrorism or imprison it with right-wing, authoritarian rule. Everywhere there was mistrust of the future, and money was running away with fear—mostly to America for some answer which was simply another form of evasion.

Their only hope lay elsewhere, in a united Europe. The first elections to the European Parliament were to be held next year. And he, Luigi Lazzaroni, was being asked to run for a seat. If the Parliament lacked federal authority, they would eventually obtain it. There was the future. There was the way to strengthen Europe and its nations—and to free Italy from its terrorists and kidnappers.

Aurelio Manzoni, waiting in his home, had a tall drink of Scotch and recalled the first time he had seen America, during World War II. He was a prisoner of war, en route to an internment camp. When his train came to Detroit, he saw a million lights blazing through the night, and he knew Mussolini had been an asshole. Who could wage a war against such a nation?

Italians had an infinite capacity for self-deception. It was a national disease. Everyone lived in a self-built world of illusion. Everyone had his own private cloud. Maybe you needed a little cloud occasionally, in order to survive. But as a permanent residence, it was slow suicide.

The foreign press was filled with stories about Italy in chaos. *Der Spiegel* had a cover showing a pistol on a plate of spaghetti. *Time* and *Newsweek* made it sound like Italy was about to sink into the sea while singing "O Sole Mio."

The nation needed a man like John Kennedy, to awaken in Italians the belief and the hope that had been wasted and embittered by that idiot, Mussolini. Such a man existed somewhere in Italy, waiting for his hour—as they were now waiting for Paolo.

ANNA TRIED not to think about what would happen if they never called and he never came home. She made preparations for the Easter party, ordering eggs and coloring, cakes and candies, party hats and gifts for the children. Maybe this year they could have a white bunny pop out of a box on the table.

He would love that. He would laugh and hold her hand. And he would hold the children, too, kissing them....

Afterward, they would take a trip, maybe to America. She would ask him for it then. She had been dreaming about it for so long and it wasn't much. Just a little piece of land, somewhere in America, with a cow. That was all. A little bit of land, a small house to hold them all when they wanted to go there ... and a cow to make milk.

He would laugh and say it was silly, but it was what she wanted more than anything else—except his arms around her.

WEDNESDAY
The 17th Day

T WAS in the evening when he heard them entering the room—both men. Then he heard Pippo speaking to him.

"Get up, Paolo. Let's go."

So this was it. As he had expected, it was to happen at night. Now he would know how it would end. If it was going to go the bad way, Pippo wouldn't do it. Not Pippo.

"You need help?"

"No thanks."

Standing up, he felt a bit unsteady.

"Where's his tie?" asked Pippo. "We can't have him look like a bum."

That was a good sign. Then they removed his handcuffs and gave him his jacket, his wallet, driver's license, identity card, and briefcase—another good sign. If they were going to kill him, they would not have given him the papers.

"You take him," said Pippo.

"Okay," Basso said. "Feel my back, Paolo? Come on, hop aboard."

In that manner, Paolo riding piggyback, they left the apartment and began to descend the stairs. Halfway down, Basso began to swear.

"Shit, you weigh more than a hog."

"Paolo's no hog!" cried Pippo, protectively. His squeezed-up voice struggled in saying the word for pig, *maiale*—going up and down as though climbing over a crooked sty.

"I didn't say he was a real hog," replied Basso. "Just try and carry him yourself."

They put him in the back of a car, on the floor, and started off. It was an old car this time, and the bumps were rough. Finally Pippo told him.

"We're taking you home, Paolo." He was so pleased with himself he almost forgot his falsetto. "Christ, I hope we don't meet any cops. It'd be one terrible disaster."

Home? *Madonna*, was it really true? Would it all be there, waiting for him? Anna, the sunlight on her shoulders, blue eyes filled with tears, Luca and Marco running toward him. . . .

"Listen," said Pippo, his falsetto in place again. "We're going to let you off near your home. You deserve it. But remember what I'm going to tell you."

He paused as the car made a sharp turn.

"After we drive away, you can take off your bandage but don't look toward us. Look the other way. There'll be someone there watching you. You won't see him, but he'll see you and if you look at us . . . well, just make sure you don't, that's all. Walk away from us . . . in the opposite direction."

As the car slowed down, Pippo gave another warning: "At first you'll have trouble, Paolo. When you take off the bandage, you won't be able to see very well. You'll have to take it easy for a little while until your eyes get used to the light. You understand?"

"Yes, Pippo. . . . Thank you, Pippo."

The car stopped, and Pippo said, "Okay, Paolo, here we go."

They helped him out. Standing on the sidewalk, he felt Pippo's arms around him.

"I wish I could work for someone like you," he said.

The arms were withdrawn, and he heard the door slam, then the car pull away. He lifted his hands and removed the bandages.

THE SHOCK was blinding. It was night, but a light from across the street seemed to bore into his brain. He felt dizzy and leaned against a wall, then fell. For a moment he sat on the sidewalk, holding his briefcase.

He tried to focus on something but it was all a blur. Gradually, he began to see he was in a short street, almost an alley. He was next to a wall topped by a fence. But when he tried to walk, he fell down again.

For the first time, he was frightened. Now he was truly exposed. Alone, without any help, he was no longer blind—yet he was unable to see. A car could run him over. Or the police could find him and ask questions when he only wanted to reach his home.

Rising once more, he leaned against the wall, trying to clear his vision. What had happened? With bandages, he had been able to walk. Now, with them off, he couldn't stand.

Finally, holding on to the fence, he began to move along the wall. Two forms were approaching—an adult with a child.

"Come away! Hurry up! Get away from that man!"

He knew his appearance must be horrendous—staggering like a drug addict, stinking like a goat, his beard a mess, holding an empty briefcase.... Somehow, he had to get home without being discovered and taken to the police in this condition.

At the end of the fence, he found himself before a larger area—a piazza of some sort. There were lights to his right, and he turned into a blazing aura of colors and flowers. It was immense, a florist's window, big as the sky. No, not this. He turned away, walking better now.

He had to find the proper street. Pippo had said he was near his home. He saw a large sign and went up to it, gradually making out the words: B R E S C I A.... So it was Piazza Brescia. But which side of the piazza?

He turned down one street and saw another large sign: F I E R A. Yes, he was getting closer. There was a street with an island in the middle, then another one and he was staring at something that seemed familiar: His sister Pia's apartment building!

He had gone in the opposite direction from his home. Peering at the buttons, he found her name and pushed the bell.

"Who is it?"

It was Pia's voice. She sounded defiant, angry.

"It's me."

For a moment there was nothing, then her voice:

"Oh, *Dio, Dio* ... it's him."

He felt his strength going and sank down onto the doorstep—where his sister found him.

Inside the elevator, the light hurt his eyes. He closed them, placing his hands over them. The door opened and Pia led him to a dark room. For a while he sat there waiting. He heard her car leaving, and then, after a while, it came back. There was the sound of the elevator, then Anna's voice:

"Where? Where is he?"

"Here."

He forced it out, in a voice he could not recognize, as though he were someone masking his voice, as though he were Pippo, squeezing his voice into a piteous falsetto, because he couldn't help it and couldn't help the plight he was in.

"For God's sake, don't come near me. I stink."

But she came anyway, and as she put her arms around him he knew that, in the Italy of today, he was one of the lucky ones, the fortunate ones, with a home to come back to, a place of his own.

Pia began to phone other members of the family. This alerted Major Delfino who raced to the apartment—arriving before anyone else. As he entered, Paolo was still seated in the darkened room, wearing dark glasses and drinking tea. Anna sat on the floor before him, holding a platter of cheese and Lazzaroni breakfast cookies.

They both stood up as Delfino entered. Paolo shook his hand.

"I want to thank you for your help. I understand you were always close to my wife."

"Don't thank me," replied Delfino. "I'm only a major. Thank her. You married a four-star general."

Paolo and Anna laughed, but the major only smiled. Anna thought it was a sad smile.

"I'm sorry, if we seemed uncooperative. We really are grateful. You were always on top of the bandits and that hurried everything up so Paolo could come home in time for Easter with the children."

The major nodded but said no more. Anna felt she knew what was troubling him.

"So we're free now," she said. "But you're not, because there are always others like us. Will it ever end for you?"

"Someday," he replied, with another sad smile.

"You don't believe we can stop them? Do we all have to run away and leave Italy to these gangsters and terrorists?"

In the darkened room, Major Delfino looked at the tall, elegant woman and her husband with dark glasses and the scraggly beard of a blind beggar. What, he wondered, could he ever tell these two people? How could he ever explain it to them?

In Trento, four carabinieri had been wounded and a Mafia bandit killed in a shoot-out before the home of the archbishop. In Naples, they had just kidnapped the son of the leader of the Socialist party. In Rome, they had blown up the office of the interior minister. But at the same time in West Germany, the nation's highest magistrate, the attorney general, had been murdered for prosecuting the Baader-Meinhof gang. And in America it was finally revealed that, in the investigation into the murder of President Kennedy, the FBI and the CIA had deliberately lied to the President, Congress, and the American people. Then came the murder of Robert Kennedy and finally of Martin Luther King, Jr. At least in Italy, they tried to fight the Mafia.

"What do you think, Major? So many friends say we'd be better off if we went somewhere else."

"No, Signora, it's useless. Italy is like anywhere else—only more so."

TWO DAYS LATER, they had the Easter party at Pia's country home near Varese. Everyone was there, including the aunts and uncles, the cousins, and many children. To avoid the shock of seeing their father immediately upon his return, Luca and Marco had been kept at the ski school until the day of the party—with the promise that they would see Paolo at Pia's on Easter.

Anna and Paolo arrived in the afternoon. In the guest cottage, they found wild flowers on their bed with a little drawing of the cottage, surrounded by trees and flowers. Beneath it was a printed greeting: *"Welcome dearest Mamma and Papa—Luca Marco Hello."*

Going outside, they encountered a group of children playing on the lawn. Paolo watched them, turning with their shadows in the sun, and it was exactly as he had dreamed it would be.

At that moment, his son Marco, who was only three, came running up—and stopped to stare at him. Paolo's eyes still bothered him and he wore dark, wrap-around glasses to protect them from the sun.

Marco took his hand.

"Come and play with us!" he cried. "Today is beautiful! Today my father is coming home!"

Epilogue

ONE MONTH later, Major Delfino moved against Kidnap Inc.—arresting the thirty-one men and three women on his list of thirty-four suspects.[1]

It was the first of six full-scale attacks on the network. In the second, 22 January 1978, three leaders of the Calabrian *'ndrangheta* were caught with a ransom payment of $1 million in lire.

In the third raid, 17 February 1978, Major Delfino and Lt. Col. Pietro Rossi of Monza broke into a villa at Legnano, near Milan, seizing seven top Mafia chiefs or *pezzi da novanta*.[2] It was a summit meeting reminiscent of the famous 1957 gathering and subsequent arrest of sixty-three Cosa Nostra godfathers at Appalachia, New York. Its purpose was to regulate drug traffic, kidnapping, and recycling of ransom money—and to coordinate the

---

[1]The case is still to be tried in the Italian courts, and nothing in this account is to be taken as part of the legal testimony of the persons involved.

[2]*Pezzo da novanta,* or "piece of ninety," originally was an artillery term for a 90mm. cannon—a big gun after the turn of the century.

successor of Don Ignazio Scelta, seventy-one, a boss of bosses who had been murdered in Palermo two days earlier.

Three months later, Major Delfino penetrated a Milan apartment to liberate Erika Ratti, 24, daughter of a wealthy silk manufacturer. From this operation, seven persons were seized—including Antonio Scopelliti, a top boss in the Calabrian 'ndranghetta.

In a fifth raid, on May 29, the major broke into another villa at Merate, near Como, freeing a kidnap victim locked in a cell in an attic: wealthy industrialist Ermino Rimaldi. It was in time to save him from paying 5 billion lire ($5.9 million). The villa—bought with kidnap money and ostensibly a retail center for soda pop and wine—was run by Filippo Sapienza who spent 1,000 lire each morning lighting candles in church. Another seven persons were arrested from this raid.

Shortly after that, Major Delfino arrested the notorious bandit Salvatore Ugone—caught with 49 million lire ($57,000) which had formed part of a 1 billion lire ($1.2 million) ransom paid by jeweller Giuseppe Scalari.

All those arrested were suspected of belonging to the same gang that had kidnapped Scalari, Rimaldi—and Paolo Lazzaroni.

The high number of Calabrians among them, especially such important bosses as Scopelliti, further confirmed Delfino's conviction from previous arrests: The Calabrians had intermingled with Sicilians and, for the most part, were running the kidnap racket in north Italy.

The Sicilians remained important, however, in other zones—as did their relatives in America. Among those seized in the summit meeting at Legnano, for example, was a naturalized American, John Richard Livoti. He had flown from New York to Palermo, his place of birth—arriving the same day that Don Ignazio Scelta was dispatched by a .38 Special fired into his spine and brain. Livoti explained to authorities that he had crossed the ocean as an act of contrition and love—to bring a statue of Santa Rosalia to his beloved Palermo. Subsequently released, he returned to New York.

One top Mafia chief failed to show up and so avoided arrest:

Gerlando Alberti, fifty-one, known as Zu Paccare, wanted as a coordinator for Mafia kidnappings in north Italy. From various hideouts, mainly in the Turin area, he remains at large to constantly rebuild Kidnap Inc.—and to threaten the lives of men like Paolo Lazzaroni and Francesco Delfino.

AUTHOR'S NOTE

In order to withhold the true identity of Renzo and Antonio, their names have been changed and some identifying factors have been veiled or altered. Further, in compliance with military regulations governing the carabinieri, the scenario of Major Delfino has been drawn only from unofficial sources. It is rendered in a way to tell this story—of human endurance and dedication to an ideal—without violating those regulations or exposing restricted elements and procedures.